PRAISE FOR
TEACHER VOICE: AMPLIFYING SUCCE.

"It is not how much you talk, is how you talk. Quaglia does it again and shows the 'how,' the importance of actively listening to teacher talk, how to value your voice, and how to converse, create, and contribute."

—John Hattie, Laureate Professor and Director
Melbourne Education Research Institute

"Russell J. Quaglia, more than anyone, has taught us about the importance of student voice. Now, in this extremely important book, he turns his attention to teacher voice. To create the schools our children need, we need to hear from everyone in our schools, not just a few. Quaglia and Lande tell us why teacher voice is important, explain how teachers can find their voice, and describe what leaders can do to hear what teachers have to say."

—Jim Knight, Author
Instructional Coaching: A Partnership Approach to Improving Instruction

"The missing link for most quality education models has been the absence of an essential keystone—the voice of those closest to the frontline. Teacher Voice: Amplifying Success by Russell J. Qualia and Lisa L. Lande supports the work of teachers and gives them specific steps for increasing their power and their influence toward improving education. It provides a blueprint for restoring collaboration, trust, and positive action among teachers. Bolstered by current research and rich with ideas for implementation, this book covers all aspects of developing and maintaining a powerful, purposeful teacher community. This enjoyable and inspiring call-to-action is a must-read for anyone interested in proactively building active teacher connections in order to give every student a reasonable chance at success."

—Debbie Silver, Author and Co-author
Fall Down 7 Times, Get Up 8* and *Deliberate Optimism

"This is a must-read for every educator, stakeholder, and politician. With so much focus on school reform, teachers are usually not even in the same room when decisions are made. This book reminds everyone that if you want to reform education, you need the teacher's voice to do it correctly!"

Glenn Robbins, Lead Learner/Principal
Northfield Community Middle School

"Teacher Voice *speaks to all teachers who have ever felt undervalued, silenced, or unmotivated because they felt their voices were not heard or did not matter. Quaglia and Lande do an exceptional job of scaffolding educational research, personal anecdotes, and practical frameworks into this solution-focused, captivating text.* Teacher Voice *is about establishing value, building capacity, and strengthening schools through the creation of a community of leaders. A delightful must-read,* Teacher Voice *encourages schools to reassess their priorities and invest in those who have the greatest effect on student outcomes—the teachers.*"

—Lisa Gibson, K-12 Curriculum Coordinator
Dubai, UA

Teacher Voice

*We dedicate this book to our fathers **Carl "Poppie" Quaglia** and **Rick "Epa" Lande** for teaching us to use and express our voice in meaningful ways. They also taught us three rules of fishing . . . bait your own hook, clean your own fish, and that only dead fish swim with the stream!*

Teacher Voice
Amplifying Success

Russell J. Quaglia
Lisa L. Lande

CORWIN
A SAGE Publishing Company

FOR INFORMATION:

Corwin

A SAGE Company

2455 Teller Road

Thousand Oaks, California 91320

(800) 233-9936

www.corwin.com

SAGE Publications Ltd.

1 Oliver's Yard

55 City Road

London EC1Y 1SP

United Kingdom

SAGE Publications India Pvt. Ltd.

B 1/I 1 Mohan Cooperative Industrial Area

Mathura Road, New Delhi 110 044

India

SAGE Publications Asia-Pacific Pte. Ltd.

3 Church Street

#10-04 Samsung Hub

Singapore 049483

Executive Editor: Arnis Burvikovs

Senior Associate Editor: Desirée A. Bartlett

Senior Editorial Assistant: Andrew Olson

Production Editor: Amy Schroller

Copy Editor: Kimberly Hill

Typesetter: C&M Digitals (P) Ltd.

Proofreader: Dennis W. Webb

Indexer: Sheila Bodell

Cover Designer: Candice Harman

Marketing Manager: Lisa Lysne

Printed in the United States of America

Library of Congress Cataloging-in-Publication Data

Names: Quaglia, Russell J., author. | Lande, Lisa L., author.

Title: Teacher voice : amplifying success / Russell J. Quaglia, Lisa L. Lande.

Description: Thousand Oaks, California : Corwin, a SAGE Company, 2016. | Includes bibliographical references and index.

Identifiers: LCCN 2016008995 | ISBN 978-1-5063-1714-4 (pbk. : alk. paper)

Subjects: LCSH: Communication in education. | Teaching.

Classification: LCC LB1033.5 .Q34 2016 | DDC 371.102/2— dc23 LC record available at https://lccn.loc.gov/2016008995

This book is printed on acid-free paper.

SUSTAINABLE FORESTRY INITIATIVE

Certified Chain of Custody

Promoting Sustainable Forestry

www.sfiprogram.org

SFI-01268

SFI label applies to text stock

16 17 18 19 20 10 9 8 7 6 5 4 3 2 1

Contents

Acknowledgments

Thanks to the countless teachers we have had the privilege of working with around the world, and whose perspectives and voices are the foundation of what we have written. In particular, we are grateful for the contributions and feedback provided by our colleagues at the Quaglia Institute, who are always ready to offer an opinion, lend support, and do whatever they can for the good of the team. We would also like to recognize Beth Havens, who inspired us early on in this journey and encouraged us to make sure the voices of teachers are always heard. Regarding the chapter on technology and voice, we would like to give a special nod to Janet Avery, Andrew Hamilton, Dan Massimino, and Eric Nichols for their specific feedback and suggestions.

We owe much thanks to Deb Young for her unwavering dedication and incredible support in launching the Teacher Voice work and in the development of this book. She gave us honest feedback when we needed it most and was always willing (day or night) to do another proof! Deb is a brilliant and beautiful person with whom we are more than fortunate to have as a colleague.

A sincere thank you to the entire Corwin Family, especially Arnis Burvikovs for giving us the opportunity to write this book and for his support and guidance from start to finish. Arnis is not only an amazing editor; he is also a treasured friend.

Finally, we are grateful for our families that provide incredible support for the work we do. Thanks to our children, Lauren, Casey, Chelsea, Cali, Ryan, Will, and Abby, for sharing your school experiences (past and present) with us. Your voices are genuine and real, and we continue to learn so much from you.

—*Russell J. Quaglia and Lisa L. Lande*

PUBLISHER'S ACKNOWLEDGMENTS

Corwin gratefully acknowledges the contributions of the following reviewers:

Gerald Aungst
Supervisor of Gifted and Elementary Mathematics
School District of Cheltenham Township
Elkins Park, PA

Marsha Carr
Assistant Professor
University of North Carolina Wilmington
Wilmington, NC

Doug Hesbol
Research Associate
University of Denver, Morgridge College of Education
Parker, CO

Glenn Robbins
Lead Learner/Principal
Northfield Community Middle School
Northfield, NJ

Karen Tichy
Associate Superintendent for Instruction and Special Education
Archdiocese of St. Louis
St. Louis, MO

About the Author

 **Russell J. Quaglia** is a globally recognized pioneer in the field of education, known for his unwavering dedication to student voice and aspirations. Dr. Quaglia has been described by news media as America's foremost authority on the development and achievement of student voice and aspirations. His innovative work is evidenced by an extensive library of research-based publications, prominent international speaking appearances, and a successfully growing list of aspirations ventures.

Among these ventures, Dr. Quaglia authored the School Voice suite of surveys, including Student Voice, Teacher Voice, Parent Voice, and iKnow My Class. His book, *Student Voice: The Instrument of Change,* published by Corwin, is already receiving international acclaim.

In addition to founding and leading the Quaglia Institute for Student Aspirations (QISA), Dr. Quaglia also founded and currently chairs the Aspirations Academies Trust, a sponsor of primary and secondary academies in England built on his aspirations research. Most recently, he has founded the Teacher Voice and Aspirations International Center (TVAIC), dedicated to amplifying the voice of teachers for them to realize their aspirations and reach their fullest potential.

Dr. Quaglia earned his bachelor's degree at Assumption College, a master's degree in economics from Boston College, and master of education and doctorate degrees from Columbia University, specializing in the area of organizational theory and behavior. He has been awarded numerous honorary doctorates in humanitarian services for his dedication to students. Dr. Quaglia's work has also led him to serve on several national and international committees, reflecting his passion for ensuring that students' and teachers' voices are always heard, honored, and acted on.

Lisa L. Lande has dedicated her professional endeavors to advocating for teachers and students around the globe. It is her aspiration that every classroom in every school be one that she would want her own three children to learn in—a lens through which she continually measures her research, writing, and professional development efforts.

She is the executive director of the Teacher Voice and Aspirations International Center (TVAIC), an outgrowth of the Quaglia Institute for Student Voice and Aspirations. The mission of TVAIC is to amplify teacher voice to enhance the aspirations of all.

Dr. Lande currently serves as a board member for the Aspirations Academy Trust in England and is engaged in a number of research and writing projects on the topic of teacher voice and aspirations. She earned her doctorate in curriculum and instruction from Boise State University and was a James Madison Fellow at Georgetown University.

Prior to TVAIC, she worked with state departments of education across the country in partnership with a U.S. Department of Education funded content center, directed a statewide reform effort, and engaged in a wide variety of consultancy roles at the international, state, and local levels on education topics, including systems reform, standards, assessment, and instructional strategies that promote individualized learning and achievement for all students.

Dr. Lande's roots are in teaching, having taught at both the high school and university level. She still considers herself to be a teacher at heart, and finds it a great privilege to partner with amazing educators around the world who are hard at work creating conditions where teachers and students can achieve their dreams.

Introduction

Many go fishing all their lives without knowing

that it is not fish they are after.

—Henry David Thoreau

The ice has finally left the lake, the sun is peaking over the edge of the ridge, and the mist from the cool crisp air is rising slowly. Four months of preparation have crept by. The lines have all been changed, the reels have been oiled, new flies crafted, licenses purchased, and books and magazines poured through in the hopes of acquiring a new skill that will lead to greater success. The L.L. Bean attire received for Christmas fits perfectly—ready in full gear! The anticipation is palpable. It is time to begin another fishing season!

"Right cover, wrong book?" you're wondering. No. This is wholeheartedly a book about teacher voice. It just happens to be written by two people who, in addition to being teacher voice advocates, are avid fishermen. (More accurately, one fisherman and one fisherwoman!) The connection and charm for us is that teacher voice and fishing involve the pursuit of something elusive, but attainable; both involve a perpetual series of occasions for hope, optimism, and endless potential.

The similarities between fishing and teacher voice are straightforward. They both require

- Time and patience—neither fostering teacher voice nor landing your limit of fish is a speedy process.
- Knowledge—you need to know what you are doing in order to achieve worthwhile results.
- Preparation—if you are not prepared, you will become easily frustrated.
- Persistence—not every effort will be successful, no matter how hard or how long you try; but can you learn something valuable from every attempt?

- Satisfaction—when done correctly, the results are amazing, and the sense of accomplishment unmatched.

And just like telling fish tales, you can even brag to your friends about your accomplishments! But at the end of the day, when done properly, there will be no need to tell tales; the truth will speak volumes.

As fisherman come in all shapes, sizes, skills, and years of experience so do the readers of this book. Although the book is titled *Teacher Voice*, it is for everyone in the school system. If teachers are to have any kind of voice they need the support, guidance and encouragement of others. Specifically, the administration, students, parents, and community members are all critical if teachers are to fully capitalize on their voice. As you read through this book there will be implications for *you*, regardless of your role in the system. Teacher voice never exists in isolation and thus the need for everyone to understand the dynamics that support and discourage teachers from using their voice is paramount.

Throughout the book, we will be sharing data and insights from a variety of sources that demonstrate the importance and effectiveness of utilizing teacher voice, including results from the Quaglia Teacher Voice Survey that has been administered to over 12,000 teachers. However, before delving in, it is important to understand *why* teacher voice is so important:

- Teachers who are comfortable expressing honest opinions and concerns are four times more likely to be excited about their future careers in education.
- When teachers have a voice, they are three times more likely to value setting goals and to work hard to reach those goals.
- When teachers have a voice in decision making, they are four times more likely to believe they can make a difference. They are also three times more likely to encourage students to be leaders and to make decisions!

(QISA & TVAIC, 2015)

Teacher voice is more than a mere vocalization of ideas; it is the use of voice *for the benefit of others and the school as a whole*. To be used effectively, teachers must listen *at least* as often as they speak, put more energy into learning than trying to convince others, and lead by taking action in a way that respects various ideas and keeps in mind the best interest of *all* who are involved.

Clearly, there are important reasons for teachers to have a voice. But we want to acknowledge up front that this has its challenges, because only:

- 59% of teachers are comfortable expressing their honest opinions and concerns
- 48% of teachers believe they have the skills to effectively communicate in their school.

- 60% of teachers think principals are willing to learn from them
- 53% of teachers report having a voice in decision making at their school

(QISA & TVAIC, 2015)

There is indeed room for improvement. If teacher voice is to be fully realized in schools, a few critical dynamics need to be in place:

1. Teachers need to feel their voice matters and feel confident expressing their ideas and opinions in a safe environment.

2. Individuals whom teachers work with (colleagues, administrators, parents, and students) need to be willing to listen to and learn from what teachers are saying.

3. Teachers (and everyone else in the school!) must be prepared to work collaboratively to take action in response to what has been learned from teacher voice.

These dynamics are reflected in the three basic principles that make up the School Voice Model. (For those of you anticipating the fishing connection, sorry, it is not Hook, Line, and Sinker!) It is Listen, Learn, and Lead. The School Voice Model, explained in Chapter 1, represents a process of listening, learning, and leading that allows you to use your voice in a manner in which it is heard, respected, and recognized as advocating for meaningful improvement in your school.

In Chapter 2, we further explore the importance of teacher voice and demonstrate the impact it can *and should* have on the entire educational community. Focal points include significant connections between teacher voice and teacher retention, innovation, professional development, and student motivation and achievement.

We have learned, sadly, that teacher voice is not yet a natural occurrence in schools. For teacher voice to have meaning and impact, one must be purposeful in expressing one's voice; teachers have the responsibility to share their voice in a way that is articulate, informed, and respectful. However, teacher voice can only flourish as a positive influence if the organization is prepared and willing to listen and learn. Chapter 3 presents various pathways to teacher voice, highlighting the importance of the Guiding Principles of Self-Worth, Engagement, and Purpose.

Chapter 4 goes into depth about the various types of teacher voice. Not all voices are heard equally . . . some teacher voices are listened to, while others are ignored. We discuss various types of teacher voices, as well as which ones have a greater impact in schools—and why.

Underpinning the importance of teacher voice is the belief that we can all learn from teachers' insights and experiences. Teachers are the foundation of schools, the ones who work directly with students and have the greatest opportunity to impact students. Certainly, they have a great deal of insight into what works, and what does not work, in schools—for themselves and for students. Chapter 5 provides an in-depth look at how teacher voice can inspire and positively (or in the absence of inspiration, negatively!) effect their colleagues, administrative leaders, parents, community members, and above all, the students.

We believe teacher voice is a powerful, yet extremely underutilized, tool in education. Technology can help change this; it has opened communication and collaboration channels for teachers to use their voice in ways that could only have been dreamt of previously. When teacher voice is respected and fostered, technology provides opportunities to enhance the impact. Chapter 6 takes an extensive look at this.

Finally, in Chapter 7, we bring the research and teacher voice work back to *you*. The potential of your voice is limitless, and the potential impact is profound. The challenges provided in this chapter encourage you to think and act differently: to lead in a way that will make a noticeable difference not only in the lives of your students but in your own life as well.

Along with the data derived from the Quaglia Teacher Voice instrument, data from international sources such as the Programme for International Student Assessment (PISA) and the Gates Foundation will be referenced throughout. Some of the best teachers we have ever worked with have graciously shared their experiences as well. Their voices are a critically important component of this book, demonstrating not only how they made a difference in schools but also sharing the challenges they faced along the way. Each chapter includes examples and suggestions for promoting and fostering teacher voice in schools. At the end of each chapter, a reflective section allows teachers to consider where they are in the process of making sure their voice is heard, respected, and valued. Rest assured, there will also be some fishing thoughts sprinkled throughout to further contemplate the important connection between fishing and voice! Our goal is for teachers to become confident in using their own voices and simultaneously realize that teacher voice, like fishing, is an art from which a great deal can be learned about life, including who you are as a person and professional.

> There will be days when the fishing is better than one's most optimistic forecast, others when it is far worse.
>
> Either is a gain over just staying home.
>
> —Roderick Haig Brown, *Fisherman's Spring*, 1951

It is more essential than ever that the voices of teachers are heard, understood, and responded to. Policy makers need to hear teachers' ideas and understand the impact these ideas can have in schools. Above all, teachers need to model for their students how to use their voice to make the world a better place so that, ultimately, they will as well.

We are asking teachers to start a revolution. Stand up and be heard! Sitting idly and wishing, longing, or hoping for change is not effective. Teacher voice, on the other hand, can make change happen. It may not be easy, but it will be worth it.

CHAPTER 1

Are You Going to Make Me Use My Teacher Voice? YES!

Be the voice you want others to hear.

For over thirty years, we have been advocating that student voice must be at the core of reform in education, if reform is to be meaningful. It has not been an easy road, and there were certainly stumbles along the way. But each positive step, and each setback, ultimately confirmed that we are right; we must listen to students, for they have something to teach us. *And so do those who teach them . . . the teachers!* For positive changes to occur in schools, everyone and anyone who is truly committed to making a difference must listen to students *and* teachers.

One of the most significant lessons we have learned is that teachers must feel their own voices are valued before they can be expected to promote the voices of students. We have discovered through our research that when teachers have a voice in decision making, they are three times more likely to encourage students to be leaders and decision makers. We have come to realize that teachers must become skilled at exercising their voice in order to support their own aspirations, as well as those of their students. For too long we have assumed that teachers, as adults who have been trained in education, are naturally strong communicators. Certainly that may be the case in many instances, but the vast majority of teachers have not *utilized* their voice to its fullest potential.

The importance of teacher voice may seem like a simple concept to grasp, and one could assume that teachers would be sharing their voices from the rooftops because they *do* have something to say. But you would be wrong. Only 48% of teachers report believing they have the skills to effectively communicate in their school (QISA & TVAIC, 2015). In addition, only 60% of teachers think their principals are willing to learn from them. Put these together and you get an unfortunate picture: We are expecting teachers to have a voice when they are not yet prepared, and don't feel invited, to share it.

Teachers and students are the fabric of our schools. If students are the heart, then teachers are the lifeblood—the critical element that keeps everything alive. Not surprisingly, student voice and teacher voice share similarities and are inherently connected. We believe that when student and teacher voices work collaboratively, there will be a shift in how educational communities work, and there will be a profound impact on the personal, social, and academic development of students and teachers alike.

Whatever Teachers Do, It Is Better With Students

We believe teachers and students share a very special relationship when it comes to voice in three significant ways:

1. *They provide the "insider's" perspective of what is working and, just as valuable, what is not working.*

What is more valuable to success than understanding the experience of those involved in the endeavor? Perhaps nothing. Successful companies recognize the value of this. They conduct feasibility studies all the time. Stores provide surveys to their clients; they even entice them to participate by providing discounts or a chance to win cash! Organizations conduct focus groups with their target audience to assess their needs.

What do they do with the feedback? They listen to it, they learn from it, and they take action based on what they learn. All this is done with the goal of meeting the needs of the clients and creating the best experience possible for them. Should it really be any different for schools? Schools serve the world's most important clients—today's youth. The purpose of schools is to meet the needs of these clients and prepare the students for life. Studies suggest that the single factor with the greatest impact on students' success in school is teachers (Hattie, 2003). Teachers are the professionals trained to serve the school's clients. Students and teachers are the fabric of the learning environment. To understand how effective your organization is, it only makes sense to ask those with firsthand experiences what their needs are and how well you are meeting those needs. The first step is to ask. It is that simple. Well, it's that simple to get started!

TEACHER VOICE

A school I was teaching at brought in a new Director. It was a good school and there was much to be proud of, but it was clear he wasn't impressed. Instead of pushing his will on the school, he put everyone in a room and asked us what we thought of our school. We generated pages of ideas. Although he'd already identified many things he wanted to change, he used this exercise to find common ground, tackling those areas first. Soon, the direction was articulated. People were encouraged to reflect on whether this was something they wanted to be a part of; some people left. New positions were created in the school, creating growth opportunities. Teachers who chose not to apply for these posts were brought on to interview panels, creating further growth opportunities. Voices were heard. People grew. The school changed.

Ole Bernard Sealey
High School Humanities Teacher
The Universal American School
Dubai, United Arab Emirates

2. *They have been largely unheard in ways that are meaningful and productive.*

While in recent years social media have led to the perception of increased teacher and student voice, it is often far too superficial. It is not enough for students to be heard when they attract media attention (good or bad) or when a post goes viral. It is not enough for a teacher to share his or her opinion online, at a staff meeting, or in the hallway. Rather, consistent opportunities must be provided for teacher and student voices to be heard *and acted on*. There needs to be an increase in the *genuine influence* of teacher and student voice in education. Teachers and students need more than an opportunity to voice their ideas, they need a seat at the decision-making table—real opportunities to influence the learning environment of which they are the most essential components—indeed, the reason schools exist at all!

One could argue that teachers have numerous vehicles to share their voice. Faculty meetings are a seemingly obvious place, most teachers are part of a union that will readily represent them, and teachers may publish their ideas in various educational journals, reaching an even wider audience. Unfortunately, however, faculty meetings are not always the most conducive place to exchange ideas or meaningful dialogue, many teachers would argue that teacher unions do not represent their ideas at all, and publishing can be a daunting process. While we recognize that no school is perfect, we are of a no excuses policy. Whether faculty meetings and unions at your school are ideal or not, there are a few underlying principles that can be fostered in schools that will promote and honor teacher voice. (And it is important to note that teachers and administrators share equal responsibility in the process.)

TEACHER VOICE

For me "teacher voice" is not about talking or about being heard. It's about entering the larger conversation. It's about wrestling with ideas and ideals. It's about reflection. And it's about change. Unfortunately, too many of us are in egg-carton isolation, alone in our classrooms, waiting for an invitation to engage. We aren't a part of the dialogue of dreams. In my early years as a teacher, I worked with some dynamic experienced teachers who sought me out. They valued my insights. They invited me to spend time outside of the pressure cooker of the regular school day, often over a glass of wine or a cup of coffee. Those conversations framed (and probably continue to frame) my thinking about teaching and learning.

Shirley Rau
High School English Teacher
39 Years Teaching
North Star Charter School
Eagle, Idaho

3. *They can be fostered through the development of the 3 Guiding Principles: Self-Worth, Engagement, and Purpose.*

Self-Worth. For students and teachers to have a meaningful voice, they need a sense of self-worth. They need to feel accepted in the school community for being a unique individual and appreciated for the contributions they make. In short, they need to feel valued.

Data show us that only 74% of teachers feel they are valued by the school community (QISA & TVAIC, 2015). It could be argued that one of the greatest roles of a school leader is to instill confidence in his or her staff and let them know that they are valued as professionals in the schools' community. It is similar to a coach getting the team prepared for the big game. The coach tells the players how incredibly talented they are and how there are a lot of people who believe in them. At game time, this comes in the form of a pep talk, ending with "Now get out there and win!" But the reality is that the players' self-worth is fostered daily, starting on the first day of practice, coming in the form of encouragement, acknowledgment for success, productive feedback when mistakes are made, and appreciation for the players' contributions to the team. The pep talk only works because self-worth has been fostered along the way.

In schools, students and teachers' self-worth is fostered when they are appreciated for who they are and the impact they have on their peers, each other, and the school community overall. School conditions need to be created that allow every individual to feel like a valued member of the community who truly belongs, while recognizing and celebrating each person's uniqueness. Teachers will feel confident sharing their ideas when they feel accepted for who they are, even when disagreement exists. While everyone does not need to be in perfect agreement (in fact, healthy discourse from differing perspectives is fuel for growth), everyone should concur that various points of view will be listened to and considered respectfully. When self-worth is fostered, teachers will see that their voice is honored, that they are respected for who they are, and that they make a valuable difference in the school community.

While principals should certainly serve as role models of respect and appreciation for others, the responsibility of creating an environment where teachers are encouraged and feel comfortable sharing their ideas does not rest solely on the principal's shoulders. Staff members need to value and respect the opinions of their colleagues, as well. Surprisingly, only 71% of teachers reported that staff members respect each other (QISA & TVAIC, 2015). When all the adults serve as models of respect and work to make their colleagues feel appreciated for their impact on the school community, everyone will benefit—including the students.

Engagement. In addition to developing self-worth, conditions in schools must promote meaningful engagement. Countless books and studies promote the importance of student engagement in the classroom. However, the primary driving force behind the engagement of students is the engagement of their teachers, which is not addressed nearly as frequently. An engaged teacher is enthused by the subject matter, motivated by the sheer presence of a student, and driven to share knowledge in a variety of ways. The passion of an engaged teacher is infectious, drawing students into their own engagement in class. The result is an improved learning environment where students and teachers alike are more motivated to achieve their aspirations.

Enjoyment of learning can impact motivation. Encouragingly, we found that 99% of teachers enjoy learning new things. Stark in comparison, however, is the finding that only 54% say meaningful professional development opportunities exist in their district (QISA & TVAIC, 2015). Teachers are ready and willing to learn new things—new ideas that will enhance their engagement and effectiveness in the classroom. But the passion of teachers will be stifled if schools do not provide them with relevant opportunities! How can schools afford *not* to provide meaningful, engaging professional development? Teachers are thirsty for it, and the impact is multifaceted. Professional development that is relevant to teachers not only provides them with fresh ideas and resources to utilize with students, but it provides another venue for collaboration, for sharing their voice. Teachers will be motivated to use their voice, and use it well, when they believe it is going to enhance their students' learning. Teacher voice will only matter when the schools create and encourage an engaging professional learning environment.

Purpose. Engaged teachers who possess a strong sense of self-worth also need a true professional purpose. The purpose is layered, because there are goals established by schools that teachers strive to achieve, as well as personal goals that teachers establish. These goals are distinct, yet overlapping, and ultimately come together to strengthen a teacher's sense of purpose.

Teachers with purpose take responsibility for who they are and what they stand for as educators. Teachers with purpose are confident, responsible, and contributing members of the school community. They exude confidence but are not arrogant. They are strong but not overbearing. They are opinionated but not blinded by their own perspective.

Sadly, only 59% of teachers say they are comfortable voicing their honest opinions and concerns with others at school (QISA & TVAIC, 2015). Almost half of the teachers surveyed are fearful of expressing their voice! Teachers who are unable to articulate their voice in matters that directly impact their purpose in school will not achieve their full potential. That is a hindrance to everyone—teachers, students, and administrators alike.

When a teacher's sense of purpose is clear, and the teacher is able to articulate and act on that purpose, the impact is priceless. Not only does the teacher's motivation and commitment have a direct effect on the teaching and learning environment, but the teacher is poised to serve as a model for students. Teachers with a true professional purpose are also better prepared to foster a sense of purpose in their students, helping them take responsibility for who they are and what they want to become.

WHY STUDENT VOICE AND TEACHER VOICE MATTER

- Offer an "insider's" perspective on the state of various aspects in the school
- Establish a sense of belonging within the school community
- Advance collaboration and mutual engagement between students and staff
- Provide leadership opportunities
- Encourage greater personal responsibility, as well as a sense of responsibility for the well-being of the school overall
- Promote curiosity and creativity
- Stimulate innovative problem solving

We have been encouraging teachers for years to foster student voice—to guide students in using their voice to build relationships, become engaged in learning and life, and develop a sense of purpose and responsibility. We have come to understand that this cannot be fully realized without teachers themselves experiencing the very same thing: opportunities to develop and utilize their own voices in an environment that respects and supports the process. It is like asking someone who has never been under water to teach someone how to scuba dive! We believe that if the voices of students and teachers are to be recognized and valued, there needs to be a shared understanding of what having a voice really means, and what it does *not* mean.

Let's start with the latter. Teacher voice is *not* about simply saying what you want and receiving it. That is called "getting your way." Teacher voice is more complex than that. Too often, we hear that the reason teachers feel they do not have a voice is because nothing happens when they offer their suggestions. First off, teachers must be sure of two things: (1) Their suggestions are communicated clearly, and (2) the suggestions can have a meaningful impact in the school. Even the most innovative idea can fall flat if it is not communicated clearly. And let's face it, not all ideas are great. That does not mean they shouldn't be shared—they should. Part of brainstorming is sharing without judging. You never know which idea will lead to valuable discussions about meaningful change. One idea prompts another and the collective conversation typically leads to an end result much different and richer than any individual thought would have produced on its own. Not every idea is spectacular or even good enough to be implemented, but all ideas have the potential to positively impact the eventual outcome.

Teacher voice is *not* about being a member of the teachers' union. Many people think teachers have a voice because they are represented by a strong union, capable of making a point using a collective voice. Good teachers' unions can and should represent the voices of teachers, but we are talking about individual teachers being comfortable and confident sharing their own thoughts and views about the teaching and learning environment.

Finally, teacher voice is *not* strictly about having the opportunity to talk. Listening is an integral component of teacher voice. No one should talk so frequently that they lose the ability to hear the voices of others. Teacher voice is *not* about controlling a situation but rather being a willing, collaborative participant in the process.

So what *is* teacher voice? It is being able to speak openly about your opinions, ideas, and suggestions in an environment that is driven by trust, collaboration, and responsibility. Teacher voice is about *listening* to others, *learning* from what is being said, and *leading* by taking action together. There are no age or experience requirements for teacher voice! In fact, the more varied, the better.

The teacher voice we are advocating for *is* utilized for the benefit of all, not just those who are the most vocal or persistent. When teacher voice is used effectively, teachers listen at least as often as they speak, put more energy into learning than trying to convince others, and lead by taking action with the best interest of all concerned in mind.

TO FLOURISH, TEACHER VOICE NEEDS . . .	
MORE:	FEWER:
Opportunities to communicate with one another	Moments of isolation
Open and honest dialogue between colleagues	Conversations behind closed doors
Professional development that addresses communication and collaboration techniques	Professional learning days focused on items that have little or no impact on learning or the culture of the school
Listening	"Discussion" with the goal of convincing
Willingness to learn from others in the present	Outdated opinions and habits of behavior based on the past

A Model for Understanding Teacher Voice

Unquestionably, when teacher voice is successfully fostered, it is intertwined with the voices of various stakeholders in schools. Ultimately, the progression of our work on student, teacher, and principal voice has led to a model that illustrates the dynamic nature of voice in a manner that is applicable to all. The School Voice Model (Quaglia, 2017) represents a process that allows teachers (and students and

FIGURE 1 School Voice Model

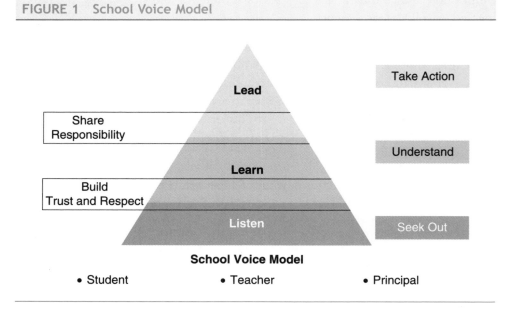

principals) to develop their voice in a way in which it is heard, respected, and recognized as advocating for meaningful change in school. As the diagram demonstrates, even when leading, you must continue to listen and learn. (Figure 1)

There are three major components to the School Voice Model: Listen, Learn, and Lead. As illustrated, there are no distinct lines delineating one component from the other. Instead, they build off of and merge with one another. Although most people conceptualize voice as being all about leading, we believe it has more to do with listening first and remaining willing to learn from others.

LISTEN

Listening is more than hearing someone; it is not a passive act. Effective listening requires outreach, openness, and a genuine interest in understanding the thoughts and ideas of others. To truly listen, teachers need to seek out the opinions of those around them. This can be a challenge, because the key is to seek out voices that are dissimilar from your own. For many, that is an intimidating undertaking. Nonetheless, it is essential. Nothing builds a deeper sense of mutual respect than genuinely listening to and considering the differing viewpoints of others. The overwhelming challenge in this stage of the voice process is teachers' own inability to communicate well with others. Only 48% of teachers think they communicate effectively in schools (QISA & TVAIC, 2015). This important issue is addressed further throughout the book.

Listening involves more than your ears; you must also listen with your eyes. Take note of when you see students engaged or disengaged from learning. If you notice that a colleague is happy, upset, or frustrated, ask why and what you can do to better support him or her. Observe parent participation and determine which opportunities elicit the most enthusiasm. How can you capitalize on what you have seen and heard in order to show parents you value their opinions and ideas? When you read about local companies that give back to the community, reach out to them for opportunities to collaborate. "Listen" to others by following educational topics on social media (elaborated on in Chapter 6). For example, #satchat is an opportunity to learn about what others believe is important in education.

Sadly, listening has become somewhat of a lost art. (People seem to be invested in a disproportionate amount of talking!) But to be effective with their own voices, teachers must first be willing to make the effort to listen to the voices of others. And while it is imperative to do within a school, it should not be limited to within the building. Listening to the voices of others beyond the school walls—within the larger community, including globally—expands the capacity to learn.

It is so important to hear what all staff members have to say. Every Thursday afternoon we have a staff update. We use a Google form to collect all voices. No one person owns the staff update, anyone can contribute and this input leads to meaningful conversations. Anyone can also contribute to professional development. We listen to each other and co-construct solutions to problems or explore things we are interested in learning about. We have a very open culture of learning and are very intentional about creating and fostering effective teams. We don't leave it to chance.

Sarah Martin
Foundation Principal
Stonefield Schools
Auckland, New Zealand ■

LEARN

As a teacher, listening needs to be more than a polite gesture or the socially appropriate thing to do. We are in awe, in an unfortunate way, of the number of open forums we have attended where a myriad of wonderful things has been said, yet nothing was really learned. It is as if attendance itself at the forum is sufficient. Far from it—listening is a great first step, but the true value of listening is in *learning* from what you heard.

Underpinning the learning, and the successful development of teacher voice, is the fundamental belief that people around you have something to teach you. Regardless of age or years of experience, the people you work with (and teach) embody expertise. Use your voice to raise questions that lead to deeper conversations! You may learn from a veteran teacher a unique way to connect your students with the community. You may learn a new classroom strategy from a first year teacher. You may learn from support staff about a different perspective on the role of parents, because they, too, may be parents, aunts, uncles, or mentors. You may learn from students' great ideas to make the learning environment more engaging.

Like listening, learning is not a passive activity. Rather than just being present, providing undivided attention during a conversation is important. In addition, taking notes is a helpful habit. This is beneficial both for future reference (when we are deep in conversation, it seems like we'll never forget the details, but our memory banks sometimes have other plans!) and to demonstrate to the person you are learning from that you value what they are saying.

During the listening and learning process, it is important to keep in mind that personal connections are important. In the midst of the conversations, relationships are strengthened and trust and respect are established. We have found that teachers with the most effective voices have taken the time to seek out and listen to others who are not always like-minded. They are open to understanding different points of view. After listening and learning, they are able to share their voice in a way that not only represents their own opinions but those of the people around them.

Sadly, our data show that there is much work to be done. Only 60% of teachers think principals are willing to learn from them. More disheartening is that only 52% of students think teachers are willing to learn from what they have to say. There is silver lining. Remember, 99% of the teachers we surveyed claim they enjoy learning new things (QISA & TVAIC, 2015). Ninety-nine percent! That enjoyment for learning reflects an incredible potential for success with the foundational components of the School Voice Model: Learning by truly listening builds mutual trust and respect, which ultimately creates the capacity for collaboration and shared leadership between students, teachers, and the administration.

TEACHER VOICE

"I'm graduating!" A senior recently told me, "I still remember how much I loved you and my kindergarten year!" Moments like these make me proud that I'm a teacher.

Kindergarten is my passion—hence my desire to teach an all-day kindergarten program at my school. I was overwhelmed with joyful pride when the principal, Shay Davis, listened to my ideas, trusted my experience, and open-heartedly heard the research validating why this program would benefit our students. She afforded me the opportunity to follow my passion and trusted me to be the best teacher for our students. This meant more than words can say.

Tisha Vanderwiel
Kindergarten Teacher
North Star Charter School
Eagle, Idaho

LEAD

Leading is all about using what has been learned to bring about meaningful change, and it is far from a solo endeavor! Having fostered positive relationships through the listening and learning stages, everyone involved is prepared for collaboration; the notion of shared responsibility now comes naturally. When people know they have been genuinely listened to, and that their ideas contributed to the overall learning, they are much more invested in supporting others and accepting responsibility for moving forward together.

When teacher voice is at its best, all stakeholders are valued for their contributions to the learning community, engaged in the school improvement process, and committed to a purpose. Embraced with mutual trust and respect, decisions are backed by the cumulative knowledge and experiences of all involved. They are not driven by testing and accountability but rather a shared sense of responsibility for determining and acting on what is best for the school.

Using this School Voice Model, teachers will be able to advocate for change based on the unique perspectives and experiences of the entire school community. If teachers effectively listen to and learn from their colleagues, students, administrators, parents, and the community, teacher voice will become an effective tool to lead through a collaborative process. The transformation that takes place with the School Voice Model is one that not only allows teacher voice and the voices of others to be heard and valued but establishes a leadership model where all stakeholders contribute to the action plan. Of course, there are variables that can either facilitate or hinder the process. Chapter 3 is dedicated to addressing those factors.

TEACHER VOICE

The teachers at my school were given the chance to have a voice to benefit our educational community. We were asked about our personal life, our professional goals, and what type of professional development we needed or wanted. Our principal listened to our needs and I knew my voice was heard. She put me in a leadership role and gave me the chance to help others. As an educator, this made me feel that my knowledge and my professional opinion was highly valued. It gave me confidence and taught me the importance of having a voice.

Holly Bowe
First Grade Teacher
24 Years Teaching Experience
Chisholm Elementary
New Smyrna Beach, Florida

Student and teacher voices contain valuable lessons that all leaders, indeed the entire community, can learn from. Teachers need to be prepared to share, and all must be ready to listen. This is the only way to create meaningful change.

Action Steps to Foster Teacher Voice

- **Establish a Teacher Mentoring Program.** One of the best ways to promote teacher voice is to establish a culture of mutual trust and responsibility. Having veteran teachers support new teachers is a great way to accomplish this. If new teachers have someone at the school who believes in them and simultaneously supports and learns from them, then new teachers will share their voices openly and honestly.

- **Post the hopes and dreams of staff members in the faculty room.** It is unreasonable to expect anyone to listen to and learn from others in the school if they do not know each other. We are not suggesting any type of "truth or dare" moments, just the opportunity for staff members to share something meaningful about themselves so others can understand who they are as people.

- **Spend a minimum of ten minutes at every staff meeting building communication skills.** All the communicating teachers do with their students does not guarantee they will be effective communicating with one another. Teachers do not become better communicators simply because it is a job requirement; communication is a skill that needs to be learned and practiced. The topics for communication exercises do not have to be education-related—they can be about anything! The goal is to develop skills to communicate clearly and effectively.

- **Protect time, at least once a week, to meet with colleagues.** The three most pressing reasons teachers provide for why they do not listen to and learn from colleagues are time, time, and time! Recognizing the importance of teacher voice is a good start, but unless the school is purposeful about establishing time for staff to communicate and collaborate with one another, it will never take hold.

- **Create a Professional Learning Board.** Designate a bulletin board in a public area of the school where teachers can share something new they learned from a colleague. Update the board weekly. Everyone, including the students, will be impressed with how many great ideas teachers learn from each other on a regular basis!

- **Buy a notebook.** Taking notes is a great way to let other people know you are invested in learning from them. Recording what they have to say reflects back to them the importance of their ideas. We each have a notebook we walk around with when visiting schools; it is here that we capture what we are learning. Our notebooks allow us to reflect on all the amazing experiences and insights we have learned while working with others. These reflections continuously inform and drive our own actions.

Teacher Reflections

1. What do you do to let other people know you are invested in listening to and learning from them?

2. List seven things you have learned from students, teachers, administrators, and/ or parents over the past month. If you cannot readily think of at least five, we suggest you start listening more.

3. When was the last time you expressed your voice with more than ten people in a room? If you cannot think of a time, we challenge you to do just that within two weeks.

CHAPTER 2

The Untapped Potential of Teacher Voice

Your passion has the power to turn up the volume of your voice.

The political, societal, and parental desire exists, as never before, to rethink our system of schooling and build a new model that ensures equitable opportunities for all students to be ready for college, careers, and life. The potential is present to build on this momentum, and teacher voice can help make it a reality.

Complementing this desire is constantly evolving technology. The educational possibilities range from learning management systems that provide access to real-time data about student progress, to online and hybrid courses, to adaptive digital content. Pilots for new models and strategies on a host of topics from competency-based progressions, to blended learning, to project-based learning and curriculum-embedded performance assessments spur conversations about how to make the possibilities a reality. Technological tools are being refined and enhanced every day, allowing students' education to be personalized in innovative and effective ways. This will be further addressed in Chapter 6.

And success is there. There are stories about outlier schools inspiring innovation and accelerating student achievement, as well as next generation schools seeing early signs of success. However, too frequently there are also stories about schools in which tools and strategies fail to bring about the much hoped-for change—change that will lead to all students having the skills, knowledge, and habits of mind that enable them to attain their aspirations. We know it can be done; yet the majority of schools in our country are merely tinkering around the edges and reverting to the status quo.

The solution, we believe, is both simple and self-evident. It is the voice of classroom teachers that inspires innovation, sustains transformation, and ultimately, creates an environment in which students' self-worth, engagement, and purpose are actualized—an environment in which all students and teachers achieve their aspirations. Andy Hargreaves and Mel Ainscow (2015) call out the traditional top-down approach to leadership as the Achilles heel of education reform. Instead, they advocate that "leading from the middle" will build sustainable professional capital in the teaching force that will result in increased student engagement and achievement. Thus, it is imperative that we stop doing things *to* teachers, and start doing things *with* them.

In "Teachers Make a Difference: What Is the Research Evidence?" John Hattie (2003) states, "We should focus on the greatest source of variance that can make the difference—the teacher." An incredible amount of resources is put into purchasing new curricula and data tracking systems, as well as hiring consulting firms to create strategic plans for schools, with the hope of finally seeing desired change come to fruition. Yet much of this is approached with a void: the voice of teachers—the very thing that makes the greatest difference. That is simply a wrong that we must make right.

Teacher Voice Over the Years

Before we explore the potential impact of teacher voice on today's education system, let's take a glance back at teacher voice in the past. Teachers were once revered within communities as critically important—tasked with the role of shaping the future of our nation. When teachers spoke in the classroom, and in the community, they were listened to. Sadly, the status of teaching as a profession has declined.

According to national polls, only 5% of teachers believe their voices are heard at the state level, and only 2% of teachers believe their voices are heard at the national level (Fennell, 2016). The Global Teacher Status Index reports that while teachers were once held in the highest of esteem within their communities, today, only 11% of those surveyed in the United States would definitely encourage their children to pursue the teaching profession, and 24% report that they would *not* encourage their children to become teachers. The 21 countries surveyed in the Global Status Index combined ranked teaching 7th out of 14 listed professions, falling in line behind doctors, nurses, social workers, and local government managers (Dolton & Marcenaro-Gutierrez, 2013).

Andraes Schleicher, Director for Education and Skills and Special Advisor on Education Policy to the Organisation for Economic Co-operation and Development's (OECD) Secretary General, writes, ". . . most will agree that the quality of an education system cannot exceed the quality of its teachers—and that the quality of teachers cannot exceed the quality of the work organization in schools and the ways in which teachers are developed and supported" (Dolton & Mercenaro-Gutierrez, 2013, p. 10). So how do teachers feel? A recent OECD report found that two-thirds of teachers felt undervalued, and our own research has found that only 69% of teachers are excited about their future career in education (QISA & TVAIC, 2015).

■■■■ TEACHERS IN THE MOVIES

From Sidney Poitier's portrayal of an East End teacher in *To Sir, With Love*, to Joe Clark's fight to improve his school in *Lean on Me*, to Jaime Escalante's success in inspiring students in *Stand and Deliver*, teachers have been historically portrayed as heroes who were intellectually, emotionally, and morally equipped to guide and guard the future, not only of our students but of our nation. Contrast these dedicated heroes with the current portrayal of teachers and their impact in movies such as *Bad Teacher* or in parodies such as Mr. Garrison in *South Park*. Over the past two decades, there has been an unfortunate decline in the value placed on teachers, their voice, and the influence they have on individual students and society as a whole. ■

A number of influencing factors have likely contributed to this shift in the perception of the teaching profession, including political debates about standards and assessments, national economic and equity issues, and the escalation of media fascination with negative news. Perhaps the most significant factor is the rigid system in which we have imprisoned too many of our teachers. We have crafted a factory model of education for our students. Simultaneously, this system has stifled teacher performance. Instead of promoting professionalism and capitalizing on teachers as a resource, we have imposed systems that dictate policies and procedures, with little room for teacher voice. A teacher recently shared with us, "I feel so beaten down. I love my students and teaching, but I feel like a deflated balloon."

We must move from a system obsessed with testing and accountability to one that demonstrates trust and respect for teachers as professionals. Teachers have an incredible responsibility—educating today's youth to become respectful, contributing members of society with the ability and motivation to achieve their aspirations. A system that demonstrates respect for a teacher's role, values their professional opinions, and fosters teacher voice and shared responsibility will allow teachers to achieve their own professional aspirations . . . and in turn, better help students achieve theirs. It is a huge responsibility, but it is what teachers are hired to do— and something they can achieve, given the opportunity to truly have a voice and be responsible leaders.

Amid the plentiful evidence pointing to a decline in the respect and value placed on teacher voice, there are examples of teacher voice on the rise, particularly within the realm of social media. Thanks to the likes of Twitter, blogs, and various online discussion forums, a whole new world of opportunity to express one's voice exists. We believe there are lessons to be learned from teachers finding their voice online. (This will be explored further in Chapter 6.) One could even argue that there is a wider audience for teacher voice now than ever before. That is to be celebrated. The key is to turn the cyberspace conversations into action and bring teacher voice alive within the walls of our schools and communities.

Additionally, the recent reauthorization of U.S. education legislation, the Every Student Succeeds Act (ESSA, 2015), includes a number of measures to directly support increased teacher training and new opportunities for teacher leadership. It has been stated that teachers will be called on to testify during at least three congressional hearings during early implementation of ESSA. We are hopeful that local education entities will capitalize on this opportunity to grow teacher leaders and amplify teacher voice for all.

The time is right. Momentum is building for meaningful change and significant reform of our education system. But this change cannot be done *to* teachers. It must be done *with* them. Teacher input must be valued, trusted, and utilized. This cannot be a token invitation to the conversation but must be meaningful and linked to decision-making opportunities. It is essential that teacher voice is not only heard but is an integral driving force as education policy evolves.

Looking Ahead—Potential Impact of Teacher Voice

When teacher voice is embraced as a critical factor in the effectiveness of a school, the potential for addressing traditional challenges is powerful. Providing teachers a genuine voice transforms the entire school culture and has a significant impact on areas such as teacher retention and increasing student motivation and achievement. When teacher voice is alive and well in a school, we observe increased innovations in learning and improved professional development opportunities. Our research shows that teachers with voice are three times more likely to value setting goals and to work hard to reach those goals. They are four times more likely to be excited about their future career in education (QISA & TVAIC, 2015). With teacher voice, schools can improve their ability to retain amazing teachers, increase student motivation and achievement, and provide opportunities for teachers to innovate and engage in meaningful professional development.

TEACHER VOICE AND RETENTION

Teacher turnover is costly, whether it is measured by the correlation to student achievement, cost in recruitment and training of new teachers, effects on school morale, and/or relational effects on students. An increasing number of new teachers are leaving the profession within the first five years. Alongside them, experienced teachers are changing schools, or even professions, because of the isolation and lack of ownership they feel within the school. The Alliance for Excellent Education (2014) report titled *On the Path to Equity: Improving the Effectiveness of Beginning Teachers* reveals that approximately half a million teachers each year leave teaching or move, costing as much as $2.2 billion, particularly affecting schools of poverty.

53% of teachers say they have a voice in decision making at their school.

Most teachers who leave do not cite poor pay, inadequate buildings, or even challenging students as their primary reasons for leaving. Instead, they describe lack of input in decisions that impact the classroom and lack of opportunities to participate, collaborate, and contribute—in short, a lack of voice and opportunities to lead (Phillips, 2015). Listening to and valuing teacher voice is not only the most direct and cost efficient method to improving achievement, but it can also be an effective way to recruit, train, and retain teachers. It is a true win-win-win scenario, because fostering teacher voice is best for everyone involved in education—teachers, students, and administrators alike!

It is important to highlight that in an era of shrinking budgets, fostering teacher voice is not expensive. It is an investment of time—time to genuinely listen and learn from what is being said, and then take action. We believe that school systems in which teacher voice is valued are magnets for the best and brightest educators, and when considering future options, they are motivated to stay in schools where they have voice. "One of the main factors is the issue of voice, and having a say, and being able to have input into the key decisions in the building that affect a teacher's job. This is something that is a hallmark of professions. It's something that teachers usually have very little of, but it does vary across schools and it's very highly correlated with the decision whether to stay or leave" (Phillips, 2015). It makes sense! But we need to make it so.

Teachers are in the best position to provide insights into how they can effectively prepare themselves, and support their colleagues, in this ever-changing world. Inviting teachers to the conversation not only improves education but also creates a sense of belonging and responsibility within the school and overtly lets teachers know they are valued. If we want to retain excellent teachers and partner with them to bring about meaningful, lasting changes in education, we simply must engage their voices. The only way to move forward is together.

TEACHER VOICE AND STUDENT MOTIVATION

The effects of teacher perception and expectations on student motivation have long been documented in research studies as a self-fulfilling prophecy. Developing

■ ■ ■ ACTION NEEDED:
OVERWHELMED AND ISOLATED

A first-year teacher had been assigned to teach in my classroom during my prep period. Fresh out of college, he was full of ideas for lesson planning and enthusiasm for the students he would teach. His energy was infectious, and it was easy to predict his students would love him and learn from him.

As the school year progressed, I watched the grind of a traditional comprehensive high school begin to wear him down. Not only was he teaching in a different classroom every period, he was teaching three different subjects, had been assigned as the advisor for a very time consuming student club, and was required to attend monthly district meetings for new teachers (which he reported were less than helpful).

Despite these challenges, he was a masterful instructor. He built incredible rapport with his students and created an environment of mutual respect. He had high expectations for himself and his students. His lessons were engaging and students were achieving—indeed thriving.

One month before the school year ended, this teacher told me he was leaving the profession. He did not complain about the workload or the students, but shared how isolated he had felt. While he had filled out plenty of collaboration forms, the only conversations he had really engaged in had occurred while waiting in line for the copy machine. He loved his students but just could not imagine doing this year after year.

I felt partially responsible for his change of heart and reflected on what I could have done to better support him and create a sense of belonging as a colleague—to let him know he was a valued member of our school community. Over the summer, a colleague and I made plans for how our staff could more effectively welcome new teachers in the fall and better support them throughout the year. ■

a growth mindset and a sense of belonging for students is key to supporting students' perseverance toward achieving their goals.

Studies by Carol Dweck (2006, 2014) and others have shown repeatedly that teachers have significant influence on student motivation and development of a growth mindset. However, teachers who have been given no voice themselves in developing the learning culture will likely struggle to support students in realizing their full capacity as learners. Teachers who feel little sense of belonging and have no ownership in school goals become indifferent, even apathetic. They believe their actions have little value or influence. This belief can translate into classroom practices, because they demonstrate limited enthusiasm for taking ownership of their own learning and professional goals, ultimately inhibiting them from optimizing their effectiveness in the classroom . . . with the students paying the price.

1 in 4 teachers admits not knowing the goals his or her school is working on.

Conversely, when teacher voice is an intrinsic part of developing policies to support learning, and when teachers work collaboratively with the belief that all students and teachers are capable of meeting high expectations, motivation thrives. Schools must seek out and honor teacher voice, letting teachers know their opinions are valued, indeed *needed*, in order to optimize the learning environment.

When teachers have a voice in decision making, they are three times more likely to encourage students to be leaders and make decisions.

John Bangs and David Frost point out, "When teachers have a high sense of self-efficacy they are more creative in their work, intensify their efforts when their performances fall short of their goals, and persist longer. Teachers' sense of self-efficacy can thus influence the learning and motivation of students, even if students are unmotivated or considered difficult" (2012, p. 3). A teacher's belief that teacher voice is heard has a powerful effect on student motivation and perseverance in learning for teachers and students alike.

TEACHER VOICE

Good teaching includes differentiating instruction for all learners; yet, teachers do not receive that same benefit. I often wonder why teachers in my school district are not permitted to create *individualized lesson plan templates* that work for their *individual teaching styles*. I was hired for a reason, so allow me to do my job . . . this includes creating a lesson plan that is useful for my content area *and* my teaching style. I would feel more valued as a teacher if I could create my own template because my differences would be honored, just the way teachers honor students' differences.

Heather Ann Keilwitz, Ed.S.
9-12 Dance and Dance Composition
14 Years Teaching Experience
Meadowcreek High School
Gwinnett County Public Schools
Lawrenceville, Georgia

TEACHER VOICE AND STUDENT ACHIEVEMENT

Teacher voice is essential to increasing student achievement. The OECD's Teaching and Learning International Survey (TALIS) reports a positive relationship between teachers' perceptions of being valued by society and students' academic achievement. In addition, participation in decision making within the school community significantly increases teacher perceptions of being valued by society (OECD, 2013a). Higher achieving countries appear to recognize the significance of teacher voice in such areas as crafting curriculum, shaping strategies, and collaborating around student learning. It is time for everyone to make a commitment to valuing teachers and honoring their voices, which will simultaneously increase student motivation.

Utilizing teacher voice—their individual and collective expertise—leads to a much sharper and richer understanding of the strategies that are effective at increasing student achievement. Rather than proceeding with wholesale implementation of practices that show promise, teacher voice should be incorporated into the decision-making process. When teachers take an active role in evaluating and implementing strategies, the benefits are worthwhile: New ideas and practices are vetted by the very professionals who will be implementing them, and the professionals will be more invested in putting the new strategies into practice. Respecting and genuinely involving teacher voice will ultimately drive teachers to more effectively support students and increase achievement.

72% of teachers report their staff works in a collaborative manner.

When teachers have ownership in the process, they more readily share their best practices and lessons learned. Individual ownership of achievement is present when teachers have voice and collaboration for improving student results becomes the norm. This, in turn, increases what Andrew Hargreaves and Michael Fullan (2013) call the social capital of school, or the ways that teachers work collaboratively around student learning, student engagement, and increased student achievement. When teachers own the learning of their students and are valued members in creating a collaborative learning environment focused on student aspirations, teacher voice consistently makes the difference in students' academic growth. Meaningful collaboration leads to a desire for more collaboration, leading to continual growth.

TEACHER VOICE AND PROFESSIONAL DEVELOPMENT

Most simply defined, professional development is the fostering of lifelong learning for teachers. It is through meaningful, sustained professional development that deep change in practice takes hold. However, far more frequently than not, administrators function on the premise that they already know what to change—without consulting the teachers. The processes and structures of high-achieving countries incorporate an abundance of teacher voice in professional development. Teacher voice and decision making to direct their own learning generates deeper teacher engagement and commitment (OECD, 2013b). All professional development for teachers should provide opportunities for ongoing analysis, reflection, conversation, and action. This, of course, simultaneously benefits students!

As previously stated, but worthy of repeating, only 54% of teachers say that *meaningful* professional development opportunities are available to them. This is unacceptable! The next wave of promising practices and engaging pedagogies must include teacher voice as an integral part of determining what best suits the learning needs of the teachers, and the needs of their students. Professional development must be meaningful *to the teachers.*

It is critical to consider that experiences, learning styles, personalities, and levels of expertise vary within a staff. Kristine Fox (2015) suggests referring to professional development as "teacher growth and learning," while acknowledging the range of skills and knowledge of individual teachers. "As we begin to look at teacher development as teacher growth, we will realize that all teachers, in fact all humans in every profession, possess different skills and knowledge. Thus, their starting point, learning method and even application of learning will differ." Adjusting your lens in this manner emphasizes the need for teacher learning to be varied and relevant to the needs of the teachers. One single approach will not be effective for all. Fox also emphasizes the importance of principals understanding teachers as learners, noting that an understanding of adult learning will ultimately increase the sense of purpose and pride in the profession. Adjusting the professional development lens now to involve teacher voice, and thereby more effectively meet the needs of participants and their students, will lead to increased engagement in learning throughout the school.

TEACHER VOICE

The moment when I knew my voice was highly valued at my school was during one of our first Leadership meetings this school year when our principal asked my team to brainstorm possible Professional Learning topics that we (ourselves and other teachers) would be interested in learning more about. She used this initial meeting to really listen to our suggestions and derive a plan to make it happen. Our Early Release Professional Learning days are now meaningful and valuable, simply because she trusted and valued our opinions as professionals. As an educator I feel engaged, motivated, and inspired more so this year than I ever have in the past!

Jennifer M. Grant
2nd Grade Teacher
6 Years Teaching Experience
Chisholm Elementary
New Smyrna Beach, Florida

TEACHER VOICE AND INNOVATION

Teacher voice is essential for innovation in schools. Innovation, infused with teacher voice, should be an integral part of transforming the educational system. Too many well-intended initiatives have lacked exactly that. Be it blended learning, competency-based progressions, differentiated learning, or performance-based assessments—examples abound where, despite the potential benefits, initiatives not only failed to take hold but prompted backlashes within the community. Teachers must be involved in the process from the very beginning, informing decision making and implementation. The absence of this will result in failed initiatives and simultaneously endanger the potential success of future initiatives.

Look closely at schools and districts that are achieving successful transformation. A common thread will be the integration of teacher voice—teachers that are intimately engaged in the design, implementation, and redesign of innovation. In schools where teachers work collaboratively toward common goals, new initiatives are carefully analyzed for effectiveness, with teachers readily sharing insight from their own experiences, seeking advice from colleagues, citing research and readings, and discussing student work. In "A Rich Seam," Fullan and Langworthy (2014) emphasize the importance of nurturing these collaborative practices in order to move toward new pedagogies, stating "In the examples we saw of new pedagogies spreading effectively, teachers and school leaders were engaged in processes of continuous, collaborative evaluation of what worked and how to best achieve improvement" (p. 53). Similarly, our own research has shown that when teachers have a voice and are encouraged to collaborate and be creative, they are three times more likely to value setting goals with a supervisor, and then work hard to reach those goals (QISA & TVAIC, 2015). Innovation, improvement, and iteration occur quickly, effectively, and continually in environments that honor teacher voice.

67% of teachers report their school is a dynamic and creative learning environment.

Listening to, valuing, and incorporating teacher voice is at the heart of meaningful transformation in schools. Every element of the school experience is impacted, including student motivation, student achievement, retention of teachers, professional development, and the implementation of innovations. Hargreaves (1994) captures the essential nature of teacher voice in saying, "It is what teachers think, what teachers do, and what teachers are at the level of the classroom that ultimately shapes the kind of learning that young people get." If educators are to inspire innovation and sustain transformation, if they are to achieve the goal that all students are ready—whether for college, careers, or life—then everyone must realize that teacher voice not only matters but also is *critical* for optimizing success.

Inspired by the popular TV show "Shark Tank," the Cobb County School District hosted its own innovative practice grant competition for teachers to receive up to $10,000 to take their innovations from idea to action. After 110 submissions from across the district, nine finalists were selected to appear in the Cobb Tank to pitch their ideas to a team of administrators, business leaders, a teacher, and a student. Teams composed of teachers, administrators, and students pitched ideas ranging from a mobile mentoring program, to equipment for developing virtual reality 3D field trips, to an elementary school "Aspiration Station" designed for students to explore who they are and what they strive to be in life. The grants awarded totaled $89,000, and without a doubt, students and teachers will benefit from the innovations this opportunity has afforded.

View the Cobb Tank Episode at: http://cobbtank.weebly.com/

Melissa Phillips Morse, EdS
20 Years Experience in Education
Director, Instruction and Innovative Practice
Division of Teaching and Learning
Cobb County School District
Marietta, Georgia ■

TEACHER ASPIRATIONS

When we truly tap into the potential of teacher voice, teachers are much more likely to reach their fullest potential and achieve their aspirations, defined as dreaming about the future while being inspired in the present to reach those dreams. When teachers are living out their dreams and aspirations, they are better equipped to support their students in doing the same.

To help foster teachers' aspirations, we offer the Teacher Aspirations Profile (Quaglia & Lande, 2016), adapted from the Student Aspirations Profile (Quaglia & Corso, 2014). This profile presents a model of various behaviors that support and hinder teacher success. There are two key dimensions to the Teacher Aspirations Profile: Dreaming and Doing; and four categories: Hibernation, Perspiration, Imagination, and Aspiration. These categories help us better understand specific challenges teachers might experience when seeking to achieve their aspirations. Recognizing where one currently resides within the quadrants is the first step to creating an actionable plan for moving into the Aspiration category, ultimately setting oneself up for optimal success in and outside of the classroom.

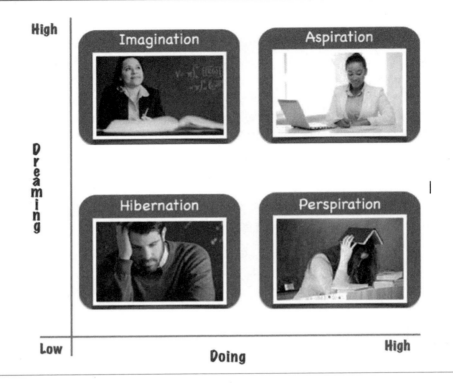

HIBERNATION

Educators who are in Hibernation have lost the passion for teaching and changing the lives of students, seem complacent (at best), and put forth no effort in the daily life of their classroom or the school community. Teachers in this category are often isolated in their own rooms, lack meaningful relationships with colleagues, and feel stuck. Minimal effort is put into lesson planning and delivery, and each school day seems to drag along at a snail's pace. Classroom instruction is boring to the instructor, let alone the students. These teachers are often described as checked-out, lazy, or simply drawing a paycheck until the next summer break or retirement. They are often characterized as unenthused or unmotivated.

PERSPIRATION

Teachers within the quadrant of Perspiration tend to work exceptionally hard on a consistent basis yet end up spinning their wheels. There is a lack of forward movement in their teaching practices and with student learning. These can be the teachers whose cars are always in the parking lot; they may be the first to arrive at school and the last to leave. They are frantically busy all the time. These teachers are often frustrated by their lack of progress and results given their tremendous effort. They may be on the edge of burnout. There is no way these teachers can work any more hours, so the lack of progress must be the fault of variables outside their control such as student background, new curriculum, or lack of time and resources.

IMAGINATION

Teachers living in the quadrant of Imagination are filled with amazing ideas and positive attitudes about the school, students, and life in general. It is easy for these teachers to enthusiastically jump aboard with every new program or project. They appear to have the "right answers" in conversations with colleagues and administrators, and they are often a breath of fresh air because they optimistically articulate the way forward for schools. These teachers speak of how wonderful current reform efforts are, how much they love all their students, and about all the new ideas they have for improving instruction in their classroom. Unfortunately, when it comes to taking action to reach these goals, teachers in the state of Imagination fall short. These teachers are described as having their head in the clouds, unrealistic, and sorely lacking follow-through. They are full of grand ideas but also empty promises.

ASPIRATION

Teachers in the Aspiration quadrant have the ability to Dream and Do. They are able to balance generating creative ideas with setting specific action steps to achieve their goals, both in the short term and the long term. These teachers are hardworking, efficient, and highly dependable. They are the ones achieving results. They willingly learn from their failures and try different approach. These teachers authentically enjoy their job and are energized by trying new things. These individuals are fully engaged in the day-to-day process of teaching and learning. Their contributions to staff conversations are honest, realistic, positive, and supportive of continuous improvement. Teachers in the Aspiration quadrant are able to clearly articulate their dreams and goals *and* follow through by committing the energy, time, and resources necessary to meet established objectives. Teachers with aspirations are equally committed to the health and well-being of the entire school community as they are to their own classroom. They view their job as a privilege and a responsibility to continually make improvements so the school can more effectively serve *all* students.

It is natural to drift in and out of all four quadrants over time. No one can live in the land of Aspiration *all* the time, or he or she would likely hit a point of exhaustion and burnout. The first step is for teachers to identify where they currently are on their personal journey to achieving their aspirations. They must determine which quadrant they find themselves in the majority of the time. Next, teachers should strive toward a balance of dreaming and doing—dreaming about the future and being inspired in the present to work hard to achieve those dreams and reach one's fullest potential. Establishing a comfort zone in the Aspiration quadrant will not only help teachers achieve their dreams but will translate into better supporting students to achieve theirs.

THE POTENTIAL OF TEACHER VOICE REALIZED

Teaching is unquestionably a noble profession, one any parent should be proud to have a child enter as a career. It is time for a return of public opinion that values teacher voice—both in and outside of schools. Teachers themselves share responsibility for making this a reality. They must be willing to share their experiences and expertise. At the same time, schools and communities must be ready to demonstrate that they honor teacher voice and are genuinely ready to listen. Conversely, teachers must be willing to listen to and learn from the community. Only when these come together, when all are willing to learn and lead collaboratively, will teacher voice be realized as the critical component of education reform that is necessary for meaningful change.

TEACHER VOICE

The biggest barrier to teacher voice is the teachers themselves. Teachers either believe they do not have anything worth sharing or are concerned about retaliation from administrators. This mindset has to change. Their everyday experiences are teachable moments that can transform the profession. Teachers should seek out opportunities to develop and use their voice. Outside of work with professional organizations, teachers can use an array of widely available technologies as a platform for advocacy, collaboration, professional development, community relations, and program promotion. The rewards to the profession outweigh the "risks" of upsetting others. If we do not tell our story, someone else will.

Julie Hiltz
PreK-5th Grade Library Media Specialist
14 Years Teaching Experience
Lutz Elementary School
National Board Certified Teacher
Lutz, Florida

Valuing teachers and their voice as professionals, both in and outside of schools, creates the opportunity to increase teacher retention, student motivation, and academic achievement. By giving teachers shared responsibility and decision-making opportunities within their school community, schools can increase the quality of professional development and inspire innovative practices. Teacher voice has incredible potential to significantly improve teaching and learning, to shape the future narrative of education.

Our research clearly tells us that when teacher voice is fostered and honored, the impact is profound. Teachers are three times more likely to value setting goals and work hard to reach those goals. They are four times more likely to be excited about their future career in education and believe they can make a difference. And the benefits, without doubt, flow into the classroom, as teachers with voice are three times more likely to encourage students to be leaders and make decisions (QISA & TVAIC, 2015).

There is a bottom line: By amplifying voice, teachers and students alike benefit immensely and are more likely to achieve their aspirations in the classroom, and in life. *That* is something we believe can be a reality for every teacher and every student in every school around the world. Nobody ever advised us to "dream small." Shoot for the moon! We think you'll like where you land.

Action Steps to Tap the Full Potential of Teacher Voice

- **Support new teachers.** Analyze your current practices and identify specific improvements that can be made to the process of welcoming new teachers into your staff, the types of support provided during their first year, and the opportunities new teachers are provided to have a voice and shared responsibility for the school community.

- **Create teacher-led improvement teams.** Select a practice, policy, or procedure (for example: school schedule, interventions, teacher duties, homework, grading policy, etc.) that can be improved at your school. Work *with others* to lead the change by gathering information about current approaches, sharing findings, proposing ideas, implementing changes, and analyzing results.

- **Collaboratively explore school trends.** Generate "Why?" and "Why Not?" lists about teaching and learning trends in classrooms and the school as a whole. Work with other teachers to identify patterns of behavior and select one or two to discuss and analyze further. Keep in mind that just because a practice has been in place for years does not make it effective. Longevity does not inherently make it a good fit, but being meaningful does.

- **Share responsibility for allocating professional development funds.** Establish a team of teachers from various grade levels and disciplines to help determine how the school's professional development funds should be allocated. Brainstorm topics that would align with the goals of the school, consider the needs of individual teachers and the faculty as a whole, and be sure teachers are part of the decision-making process.

- **Individualize professional development.** Ensure teachers have the opportunity to set goals and create their own personalized professional development plan. Meet with the building and district administrative teams to share the importance of individualized learning. Encourage all colleagues to share with the faculty what was learned and how the new knowledge can influence the work of the school.

- **Share innovative practices.** In addition to more formal professional development practices, share innovative ideas informally with colleagues. This can range from books about education, to observations made throughout the school, to ideas learned from other schools through social media. Take advantage of a variety of forums for sharing innovative practices such as staff meetings, the school website, newsletters, bulletin boards, and so forth.

- **Be a model!** Teachers having high expectations of themselves, and their colleagues, set the stage for teachers having high expectations for their students. This parlays into students establishing high expectations of their own!

- **Know your colleagues' aspirations.** Ask fellow teachers and administrators what their hopes and dreams are. Share the Aspirations Profile. Use it as a tool for recognizing current status (Hibernation, Perspiration, Imagination, Aspiration), then determine actions that can be taken to balance dreaming and doing.

Teacher Reflections

1. How do you encourage and support new teachers?

2. What practices does your school have in place to ensure your professional development needs are met?

3. What kind of opportunities are you given to experiment and innovate?

4. Which one of the Aspirations Profile quadrants do you fall into? What can you do to foster your own ability to "dream" and "do"?

5. What can you do to help others establish a comfort zone in the Aspiration quadrant?

CHAPTER 3

Pathways to Teacher Voice

It takes time to find your voice, but when you do, make sure others can hear it.

Educational research and practices clearly demonstrate that teacher voice is a critical element to school success and the ability to meet the needs of students. Teacher voice must be valued as an extraordinary resource rather than a distracting challenge to deal with or an arbitrary component of a school to be managed.

Meaningful teacher voice will not come alive in school systems easily. It cannot be declared in a mandate from central office: "Hear ye, hear ye! From this day forward all teachers shall have a voice!" Teacher voice is not accomplished via a checklist, or something that is done once and finished. While teacher surveys have a meaningful purpose, they cannot be administered simply to check the "get teacher opinions" box, believing that teachers truly had a voice. Surveys simply collect data; it is what you do with the data that matters. Likewise, a full day of professional development dedicated to teacher voice will not get the job done. Checking off the "teach teachers about teacher voice" box does not go nearly far enough. We don't need to instruct teachers on fostering voice; we need to involve them in it. What is needed is a culture shift in how the public, leaders, and teachers themselves view teacher voice and engagement in the business we call school.

Despite the potential it offers, teacher voice is often completely absent from conversations and decisions about how to improve schools. Hargreaves and Fullan state, "Where students are concerned, the teacher will always be more powerful than the principal, the president, or the prime minister. Successful and sustainable improvement can therefore never be done *to* or even *for* teachers. It can only ever be achieved *by* and *with* them" (2012, p. 45). Teachers are doing amazing things within the constructs of their classrooms, but imagine what they are capable of when invited to join in the ownership of a school, to become true partners in a journey toward improvement for all. Teachers are an untapped gold mine!

For teachers to feel confident sharing their ideas and perspectives, they need to know their voice will be valued, listened to, considered, and acted on. Teachers are not (or should not be!) looking for a guarantee that every idea will be implemented. There will always be differing opinions, debates, and compromises, as there should be, but teachers need know they are a genuine part of the decision-making process. To ask for teachers' opinions but then not respond to the information is akin to stating, "We don't care." A token inclusion is more than useless, it is detrimental to the morale of the teachers and the school environment overall.

Most school leaders and policy makers would *say* that they value teachers and their opinions; but those words must be supported by actions that back up the claim. It is a complex process to systemically shift the culture of a school from one that occasionally surveys teachers, to one that listens to and learns from the voices of teachers. As pointed out with the School Voice Model in Chapter 1, listening and learning must lead to meaningful action in partnership with others. Anthony Muhammad provides the following description of what it takes to create a substantial cultural transformation:

> Cultural change is a much more difficult form of change to accomplish. It cannot be gained through force or coercion. As human beings, we do not have the ability to control the thoughts and beliefs of others, so cultural change requires something more profound. It requires leaders adept at gaining cooperation and skilled in the arts of diplomacy, salesmanship, patience, endurance, and encouragement. It takes knowledge of where a school has been and agreement about where the school should go. It requires an ability to deal with beliefs, policies, and institutions that have been established to buffer educators from change and accountability. It is a tightrope act of major proportion. (2009, p. 16)

Sound overwhelming? Perhaps. But do not lose heart. Creating such a change is a journey, not a race.

Willingness and Readiness

Fostering teacher voice does not yet occur naturally within most schools. Unfortunately, it is not as simple as flipping the teacher voice switch to allow teachers to instantly have a productive voice in school. It is a process that takes time and energy from individual teachers and administrators; the entire organization must work together to make teacher voice an integral part of the school environment. There are two major components that must be addressed on the

TEACHER VOICE

Because I teach kindergarten, I feel like I have to use my voice to advocate for students on a daily basis. As we move toward more "rigor", the curriculum and expectations become more and more developmentally inappropriate for my five and six year olds. I have had to fight to keep both recess and "free play" time. We are being forced to use a direct instruction program for reading that does not take into account the way young children learn. While I cannot stop the county directive, I have used my voice to fight for a gentler implementation at our school. I am now on a county committee of ELA leaders. Unfortunately, I do not feel that they are listening to our voices but instead are just giving us information, no questions asked. I will continue to fight for county administration to listen to the voices of those of us actually in the classroom.

Karen Weinrich
Kindergarten Teacher
14 Years Teaching Experience
School Advisory Council Chair
Spruce Creek Elementary
Volusia School District
Florida

journey to weave teacher voice into the very fabric of a school system: Teacher Willingness and Organizational Readiness.

Both variables must be in play for teacher voice to thrive as part of the ethos of a school system. A school can be filled with willing and capable teachers who are prepared to utilize their voice, but if the organization is not ready to listen and value that voice, it will fall flat. Conversely, an organization can be fully ready to embrace teacher voice, but the potential will not be fulfilled if teachers are not adept and prepared to effectively exercise their voice. Teacher Willingness and Organizational Readiness are equally significant; this is not a sequential approach, where one component needs to precede the other. The key is that the two aspects are present simultaneously.

There is no perfect starting point for Teacher Willingness and Organizational Readiness. Individual teachers will begin with varying abilities and degrees of willingness to share their voices. Likewise, every organization will begin with varying comfort levels in regard to sharing responsibility and fully embracing teacher voice. This is natural and to be expected. It follows that each school will take a unique path on this journey, and the degrees of Teacher Willingness and Organizational readiness will fluctuate over time. Successes and challenges, as well as progress and backsliding, will occur. It is how you respond to it that matters.

The most important thing is for teachers and administrators to be simultaneously invested in making teacher voice an integral part of school change; everyone must be committed to moving forward *together*, from whatever point you find yourselves.

Even when teacher voice effectively becomes part of the ethos of the school, it must continuously be nurtured to be effective. There is no finish line; schools should never be "done" with teacher voice. Rather, schools should reach a place where teacher voice has been fully incorporated into the fabric of their system, at which time the focus becomes continuously honoring and fostering teacher voice.

When teachers are willing and an organization is ready, a system can integrate teacher voice into all aspects of teaching and learning. When this is achieved, teachers and administrators work together in an open, trusting, and collaborative culture that ultimately benefits everyone, most importantly the students!

Teacher Willingness		
Teachers have self-worth, are meaningfully engaged in the educational community, and have a sense of purpose.	**Organizational Readiness**	
	Administration is prepared to support and embrace teacher voice by providing ample opportunities for teacher input and engagement.	**Teacher Voice**
		Teachers and administration work together in a balanced manner with an open, trusting and collaborative relationship that benefits all in the system.

TEACHER WILLINGNESS

Teachers must be proactive participants in fostering their own voice. Educators in K–12 and higher education sectors need to engage their voices—all 7.2 million of them! There are currently audible voices, the loudest perhaps from teachers who wish to be viewed more favorably and professionally by the public. While we wholeheartedly agree with that sentiment, we recognize the importance of teachers reflecting on their own voices, evaluating their effectiveness and purpose, and assessing their own skill and will to use their voice.

Not unlike the students in their classrooms, teachers' personalities and attributes span the spectrum, impacting the way teachers exercise their voice. Some teachers possess a natural gift for communication and are clearly comfortable engaging in conversation with nearly anyone. Others readily demonstrate strong communication skills when working with students yet struggle with peer collaboration and public presentations. Some teachers are extroverts by nature, while others are on the shy side.

48% of teachers report that they communicate effectively in their school.

Personal attributes aside, we challenge you to find a teacher who says he or she wishes to be ignored, to *not* be heard. As humans, we all want to matter, and being heard is an integral part of that. But we cannot assume that a desire to be heard automatically translates into teachers being skilled at utilizing their voices. There is always room for improvement in the area of communication and collaboration. However, change will not occur without effort.

While numerous professions have communications requirements as part of their core training, teaching is not one of them. Be mindful that not all teachers enter the profession with the same baseline experience and comfort level in communication. Teachers should also recognize this in themselves. They must commit to developing the skills and confidence to share their voice and make a difference. Regardless of natural ways of being and built-in default patterns of communication, every individual in a school system has a responsibility to contribute their own voice, value the voices of others, and work toward a balanced, effective system of communication.

Only 68% of staff say they are comfortable asking questions in staff meetings.

For some, lack of skill is not the issue; it is a lack of will. Unfortunately, there are a number of teachers who are resisting the shift to a more collaborative model of schooling. They prefer to work independently with the classroom door tightly closed to colleagues. While various learning styles among teachers should absolutely be respected, teachers should not be able to opt out of collaboration. Research demonstrating the positive impact of teacher collaboration on student learning is for too powerful to ignore (Hattie, 2009, 2012, 2015; Knight, 2011, 2016; Fullan & Quinn, 2016; DeWitt, in press). Resistance to engaging in the school community beyond one's classroom must be addressed. It is critical that all voices contribute to important school decisions. Teachers need authentic invitations and encouragement to engage their voices in the school, coupled with support from leadership and peers.

We believe the vast majority of teachers *are* willing and looking for opportunities! When teachers are willing to utilize their voice to positively impact the school, they will continually work on effective communication, participate frequently in collegial conversations, and advocate for the profession within the community. They will simultaneously be fostering a strong sense of self-worth, become meaningfully engaged in the learning environment, and be able to articulate a clear purpose for their role in the school community.

During my fifth year of teaching third grade, I was asked by my administration to share with staff how I effectively conduct writing conferences during my writing workshop. My administrator put a substitute in my classroom and I spent one day giving a short presentation to each grade level on what they could do to make conferencing with students easier and more effective in a shorter period of time. This day of presentations lead to me coteaching a four-day Writing Workshop the following summer. The experience made me feel as though I was doing something well within my classroom that was not only benefiting the students but also the staff within my school and surrounding area.

Tamla Chambless
3rd Grade Teacher
10 Years Teaching Experience
Clarkdale Elementary School
Cobb County School District
Marietta, Georgia

ORGANIZATIONAL READINESS

While individual teachers have a responsibility to develop effective communication skills and engage in conversations beyond their classroom walls, school systems and administrators play an equally critical role in the success of teacher voice. Just as teachers have the responsibility of creating an environment conducive to engagement and learning for students, those in positions of leadership must afford the same consideration to teachers.

> *Only 60% of teachers believe that building administration is willing to learn from staff, and even fewer (45%) believe that central office understands the unique culture of their school.*

Teacher willingness to utilize their voice means little if the organization does not create an environment that fosters a collective ownership of the school. If you put an effective teacher up against a rigid system, the system will win nearly every time. Far too often, bright young teachers are leaving the profession after only a few years, or seasoned teachers (ideal mentors for new teachers!) are burning out and turning to other careers. It's a lose-lose situation. The teachers' passion is stifled and the school loses some of the best in the profession, at an incredible loss to students.

▪▪▪ AUTHENTIC SHARED LEADERSHIP . . . NOT!

A successful middle school frequently touted their model of shared leadership as a bright spot in their system. Unfortunately, the teachers disagreed. Sure, the administration sent out e-mail surveys periodically, but they rarely followed up on the results. It was clear to teachers that administrators regularly consulted with their two favorite teachers, but they appeared to disregard the opinions of everyone else.

Despite the fact that teachers were feeling devalued and ignored, they rallied well within their own space. Teams conducted various action research projects, ultimately discovering some amazing things about their school to celebrate, as well as identifying areas for growth. Teachers were energized by their collaboration and were eager to share their ideas. Unfortunately, they felt as though sharing with administrators would be a waste of time; it was easier and less disheartening to just work around them. ▪

Organizations will retain talented and committed educators when they demonstrate that they value them as professionals and that they want *and need* their input. Where do you begin? By asking teachers! Ask them to share specific ways they would like to be more meaningfully engaged. Possible first steps include inviting teachers to facilitate faculty meetings, providing staff with decision-making roles on school and district committees, and promoting open communication that includes opportunities to express dissenting opinions in a safe environment.

As stated in Chapter 2, teachers who leave the profession cite lack of input and opportunity as significant reasons. When leaders do not put forth a concerted effort in these areas, or worse yet, feign interest, the result is devalued and frustrated teachers. Seeds of resentment can grow into a negative use of voice that is detrimental to the entire school community. To avoid such a situation, organizations must genuinely embrace teacher voice and provide ample opportunities for shared responsibility within the school community.

Teachers, and their students, are at the heart of the learning environment in schools. They create its foundation and are the stakeholders most affected by change. It only makes sense that they have input into the decisions that impact their learning environment. Yes, there will be teacher voices that are challenging at times. Yes, it can be uncomfortable to navigate human dynamics and incorporate varying voices. And yes, it would be easiest to straight out dismiss difficult dealings as disheartened grumblings. But it wouldn't be right. There is something to be learned from every voice. Teachers are an invaluable resource that brings great value-added benefits to the organization, if only given the chance.

As demonstrated in the School Voice Model, the full potential of voice is realized when, within an environment built on mutual trust and respect, all members of the school community genuinely listen to and learn from one another . . . then take action together.

TEACHER VOICE

A barrier to teacher voice that I have observed from the administrative perspective is the lack of understanding exhibited by many leaders regarding what teacher voice is and what it is not. Administrators should focus on how teacher voice can effectively be included in school and district leadership models rather than fearing potential challenges. My colleagues and I, who have all sincerely embraced the concept of teacher voice, have seen an increase in learning for adults and students. It is the openness of the administrators that ensures a culture for teacher voice to thrive.

Karen L. Beattie, EdD
Principal (Former High School
Social Studies Teacher)
29 Years in Education
Chisholm Elementary School
Volusia County Schools
New Smyrna Beach, Florida

REALIZING THE POTENTIAL OF TEACHER VOICE THROUGH THE 3 GUIDING PRINCIPLES

For teacher voice to truly flourish, school systems must embrace and embed the 3 Guiding Principles that affect aspirations and voice (adapted from Quaglia & Corso, 2014):

Self-Worth—Teachers need to feel accepted for who they are within a safe environment where varying ideas are respected; they must have a colleague who is a hero, someone they trust and can turn to as a mentor; and they must feel a sense of accomplishment for their efforts.

Engagement—Teachers must be meaningfully engaged in a teaching and learning environment where they enjoy what they are doing, can be creative, and are willing to take risks without the fear of failure or success. Yes, this means they should have fun on the job!

Purpose—Teachers need opportunities to take on leadership roles; they must have the opportunity to conduct themselves as the professionals they are, apply their skills and knowledge, and accept responsibility for their actions; and they must have the confidence to take action knowing that what they are doing will benefit those around them. This Guiding Principle is arguably the most difficult to ensure yet the most important to implement.

To create the conditions necessary for students to achieve their aspirations, teachers must be on their own professional journey—one that allows them to achieve their full potential. Teachers must be able to dream about the future and be inspired in the present to take action to achieve their aspirations. To accomplish this, teacher voice must be honored and responded to—on an individual and collective level. The teachers and the school as an organization have mutual responsibility in this journey.

ASSESSING TEACHER WILLINGNESS AND ORGANIZATIONAL READINESS

	TEACHER WILLINGNESS	ORGANIZATIONAL READINESS
Self-Worth	Do teachers know one another's hopes and dreams? . Do teachers work together outside of required collaboration time? Is the staff welcoming and supportive of new teachers?	Does leadership provide team-building opportunities for teachers? Are the accomplishments of teachers frequently celebrated in the school? Do leaders know the hopes and dreams of their teachers?
Engagement	Do teachers have fun within the learning environment? Do teachers actively explore new concepts, topics, and ideas they are curious about? Are teachers willing to take risks and try new things?	Does the school environment encourage teachers to be creative and have fun? Do teachers have input into the profession development that is offered? Do leaders encourage teachers to take healthy risks, and let them know they are supported whether they succeed or fail?
Purpose	Can teachers clearly articulate their purpose as educators? Do *all* teachers step up and take active responsibility for the school community?	Are teachers meaningfully engaged in setting their own professional goals? Do teachers have authentic opportunities to take on leadership roles that match their passions and interests?

The first step is to evaluate the current state of self-worth, engagement, and purpose for both teachers and the organization. The following table provides questions to help assess teacher willingness and organizational readiness in relation to the Guiding Principles.

Equipped with this knowledge, action must be taken to embed conditions that support the Guiding Principles.

BUILDING SELF-WORTH

Fostering a strong sense of Self-Worth among a teaching staff is more important now than ever. Today's role of teacher, and the expectations that accompany it, are continually being redefined. Teachers are asked to be a guide-on-the-side, facilitator, coach, and activator of learning, to name just a few. Many teachers are struggling in isolation to navigate these changes. They seek to understand and respond to new expectations, but their lack of voice and collaboration leads to frustration, further eroding their sense of self-worth. Teachers need to believe they are a valued and supported part of the school community.

Fostering self-worth simultaneously promotes self-efficacy, a fundamental belief in our own potential to have an effect, a belief in our ability to set and achieve goals. When self-worth has been effectively cultivated in a school, teachers work collaboratively to improve every element related to the teaching and learning environment—not only for themselves but also for the benefit of the school as a whole. Collegial relationships and cooperative learning communities thrive, not only in structured formats but also in spontaneous and unprescribed ways. Experienced teachers share the art and craft of teaching with novice teachers, providing assistance and advice—not only on issues directly related to students but also on the value of the profession itself. Veteran teachers concurrently learn from the ideas and fresh perspectives of new teachers. When self-worth permeates a school in this manner, teachers model for students a deep sense of belonging and shared responsibility, both to the school family and to the community as a whole. The potential impact is immeasurable.

In today's schools, however, instead of ongoing coaching, collaboration, and conversation with colleagues, teachers often have little control over their time, few opportunities to collaborate, and little input into decisions. Too frequently, teachers attend mandated meetings with predetermined topics, with little regard to whether the topics are relevant to the needs of the teachers. Mentoring relationships have become less personal and more formalized; scripted meetings have replaced conversations; and checklists have replaced personalized goals. Many teachers report that they are bogged down by volumes of paperwork, standards-based assessments, and meetings that are not adding value to their practice. Rather than developing self-worth from setting and achieving goals with personalized action plans, many teachers find their goals, and the methods for achieving them, prescribed and void of meaning.

74% of teachers believe they are a valued member of their school community. That means 1 in 4 teachers do NOT feel valued in the school community!

At its heart, self-worth has to do with a sense of belonging and the knowledge that you are valued for your unique background, talents, and skills while at the same time appreciating that you are a member of a larger group with shared goals and beliefs. Teachers are eager to contribute their individual gifts and passions to shaping the teaching and learning environment. This includes helping to define and continually improve the role and expectations of teachers, as well as engage in the process of making decisions that impact the school. Teachers are the perfect resource to guide and support school improvement efforts. Meaningful change must be informed and shaped from within—by the practitioners themselves (and their students, of course); the ones with firsthand experience.

59% of teachers claim their school celebrates the accomplishment of staff members.

To be fully invested in contributing to school progress, to be "all in", teachers, like all humans, should be appreciated for their efforts. Only 56% of teachers report they are recognized when they try their best, and 19% say they have never been recognized for something positive at school (QISA & TVAIC, 2015). Teachers are responsible for creating a learning environment where instruction and student achievement are continually improving. If we expect teachers to continually work hard at refining their practice, it is imperative that their efforts and accomplishments are celebrated regularly and frequently.

TEACHER VOICE

When I began teaching, my voice meant very little. I felt the administration did not care what I had to say. Many teachers still feel this way, and it bleeds over into how we treat students. It wasn't until I saw my colleagues struggling that I realized I may be their only support. That is one reason I chose to pursue a degree in educational leadership so that my staff will feel successful and teach our students to become successful.

Ryan Schweikhart
4th Grade Teacher
7 Years Teaching
Bodine Elementary School
Oklahoma City Public School District
Oklahoma City, Oklahoma

Failure to attend to teachers' self-worth and self-efficacy correlates with growing rates of teachers' dissatisfaction and attrition, particularly within the first few years of entering the profession. We must keep in mind that dissatisfied teachers have a direct impact on students. Fortunately, the adverse is true as well! When self-worth is fostered in schools, the result is teachers who feel they belong, can make a difference, and that make long-term professional commitments. Teachers already work incredibly hard. It's time to ensure they know their efforts are appreciated, not just by the students but by everyone in the school community.

■ ■ ■ IN ACTION: BUILDING A SENSE OF SELF-WORTH

Every year, the teachers and administrators from a national award-winning secondary school leave town for a three-day retreat. A team of administrators and teachers collaboratively plan the agenda, and they gather at a rustic camp where they spend time reflecting on their shared goals and philosophy about learning, developing the year's integrated units and activities, and brainstorming ways to be more effective in their work with students.

They also cook for each other, play games, take hikes, and spend time renewing friendships and getting to know new staff members. Around the night's campfire, they laugh, debate, and tell stories about their students, each other, and their families. They get to know one another as individuals, sharing their hopes and dreams for the future, personally and professionally.

The time and financial commitments are significant, but the payoff of a staff committed to each other, their shared goals, and their students, has proven time and again to be well worth the effort.

"I can't imagine how we could be successful if we didn't have this time together," the school's principal says. "There's no way we could build a culture of caring and community with our kids if we didn't first do it for ourselves!" ■

There are three essential conditions to fostering Self-Worth: Belonging, Heroes, and Sense of Accomplishment.

To foster Self-Worth in teachers, schools must cultivate a sense of Belonging, while also celebrating each teacher's individuality. Schools are filled with undiscovered talents residing within their teachers. When teachers and administrators really get to know one another, sense of belonging flourishes and individuals are more likely to share their talents and exert maximum effort toward productive collaboration.

Teachers also need professional Heroes; people they respect and can learn from. Every teacher needs at least one trusted colleague with whom they can share their struggles and successes. Heroes can be found within the school community or externally, but they need to be individuals who are directly and regularly accessible for support and inspiration.

65% of teachers are excited to tell their colleagues when they do something well.

It is also important that teachers experience a Sense of Accomplishment with their work. While every single effort does not need to receive applause, teachers' successes and efforts overall should be recognized within the school community. This should become an accepted and celebrated norm. Unfortunately and paradoxically, sometimes the best way to alienate a teacher is to make him or her Teacher of the Year, because colleagues may react with feelings of resentment and envy. Fifteen percent of teachers report that they are concerned colleagues will resent them if they are too successful (QISA & TVAIC, 2015). Teachers can also be humble to a fault, unintentionally thwarting opportunities for colleagues to learn from each

TEACHER VOICE

What does teacher voice mean to me?

With great power, comes great responsibility . . .

The choice to use my voice just makes sense,

and it's clear to my peers the consequence

is an environment and community

where all feel free

to express ideas openly.

It's empowering to see fellow teachers devouring

the opportunity to share, failures and success

If all teachers care, then yes!

Yes, voice is the key . . . not an iPad or a test.

Use students' first names. Say thank you.

Be the change. Don't try to fly, open your eyes, realize,

you just flew.

That's what teacher voice can do.

Tyrel Whitt
Middle School Language Arts Teacher
11 Years Teaching Experience
North Star Charter School
Eagle, Idaho

other's successes. To truly realize self-worth, open and trusting environments must be created where teachers can safely and confidently share their successes (and failures) for the benefit of all in the school community.

Self-worth will soar when teachers feel like they belong, have heroes they connect with, and experience a sense of accomplishment resulting from their hard work.

INCREASING ENGAGEMENT

Over the past decade, education systems have increasingly caved to narrow definitions of teacher success, prescribing learning through pacing guides and course sequences, and compartmentalizing professional development into predetermined and impersonal modules. What has been lost in the shuffle is the understanding that teachers should be, first and foremost, lifelong learners. Continually gaining new knowledge is at the heart of the profession. Just as is expected for students in the classroom, learning must be engaging for teachers.

Teachers have heeded the research calling for increased student engagement and opportunities for students to collaborate, think critically, and solve complex problems. It is time to audit the adult learning designed for teachers and make sure the same is afforded to them: the chance to be deeply engaged in continual learning, grapple with new concepts with colleagues, and assume greater ownership of their work. This can be achieved by allowing and encouraging teachers to craft curriculum, to ask "Why?" and "Why not?" about new approaches to improve student engagement and performance, to take risks with new technology, and to be enthusiastically engrossed in learning with students.

Only 67% of teachers believe their school is a dynamic and creative learning environment, and only 54% report that meaningful professional development opportunities exist in their district.

Too frequently, professional development neglects to foster engagement for teachers, and it fails to model anything that is either *professional* or *development*. There is a rush to deliver the latest and greatest in a one-day "lecture with slide deck" format without ever asking teachers about their professional development needs. It is somehow believed that delivering more at a faster rate to the masses is somehow better. Professional development should not be an assembly line. This disregards the synergy that is possible when teachers are intellectually, emotionally, and socially engaged in ways that are relevant to them.

The unique needs of teachers must be considered, because every group of teachers represents a diverse range of needs and ambitions for continued learning. What is the best way to determine how to best meet teachers' specific needs? The most straightforward approach—ask them. Engaging professional development needs to honor and evolve from teacher voice. Professional development opportunities should be driven by conversations with teachers about student work and learning, shared case studies and curiosity, and the individual and collective needs of teachers. It should be an ongoing exploration of the art and science of teaching, conducted in a manner that meets the needs of the teachers in attendance. Incorporating teacher voice is the most effective way to ensure engagement for teachers and an immediate impact in the learning environment they share with students. The most powerful resource for determining effective professional development resides within teachers themselves.

67% of teachers say their school is a dynamic
and creative learning environment.

It is also important that teacher curiosity and creativity be woven into professional development and regularly encouraged and rewarded in schools. As new initiatives are rolled out in schools and districts, teachers who ask "Why?" may be seen as troublemakers and saboteurs. Teachers who develop new and different strategies and classroom structures and ask "Why not?" may suffer negative evaluations because their methods and strategies do not "fit" neatly into evaluation checklists. More and more frequently, teachers talk about "playing the game" when evaluators come into their classrooms, performing cookie-cutter lessons they know will match whatever model of evaluation has been adopted by the district. Effective and meaningful evaluation systems must include curiosity and creativity as hallmarks of true engagement for teachers and students alike.

When done well, professional development can reflect the type of engagement and collaboration necessary to make a positive, lasting impact on teaching and learning. In Lorna Collier's interview of Linda Darling-Hammond, "The Need for Teacher Communities" (2011), Darling-Hammond discusses the importance of collaboration in saying, "The opportunity to share what they know with each other also allows them to be individually successful and successful as a team—and teaching is definitely a team sport" (p. 14). The more time a team has to practice with one another, and the more involved the team can be in the game plan, the more effective they are come game time.

Three conditions serve to foster Engagement: Fun and Excitement, Curiosity and Creativity, and Spirit of Adventure.

Fun and Excitement should not be reserved for students (and even then, should not be restricted to the playground!). To be fully engaged, teachers must enjoy being in the classroom. That's right, we believe that school should be a *FUN* experience for students and teachers alike: learning environments where teachers and students are so engaged that they lose track of time and space (Csikszentmihalyi, 1990). This does not mean the school day is "fun and games" in a frivolous sense but rather that an upbeat and engaging presence should permeate the school culture for teachers

A highly successful elementary school principal was asked about the key to consistently high satisfaction ratings provided by his teachers each year and to the steady gains in student achievement.

"Several years ago, this wasn't the case," he explained. "I was losing teachers every year, and morale was at an all-time low. I asked a group of teachers from each grade level to talk to me about what they were seeing, what was causing teacher frustration, and what changes we needed to make. Over and over my teachers told me that they felt they had no real input into what we were doing and where we were headed. They came up with the idea of a leadership team made up of teachers and administrators who would meet every week to look at school goals, policies, and practices. Every grade selected teachers to represent them, and part of the role of these teacher leaders was to represent their grade and to keep lines of communication open. It wasn't always easy; teachers had some strong opinions about the ineffectiveness of some of our practices, and it was hard for some of our administrators to let go of the idea that they were the sole decision makers. We are in our fifth year of using our leadership teams to guide our work, and we have seen incredible changes, not just in teacher satisfaction but also in everything from student achievement to school culture. Our teachers are leading this school; they really have ownership in every aspect of what we are doing." ■

and students alike. The teacher sets the tone for the learning environment, and if they are having fun, it will be contagious.

Promoting Curiosity and Creativity is another way to increase teacher engagement. Teachers must take action to explore things they are curious about and seize opportunities to be creative with their lesson planning and instruction. If a teacher is bored during a lesson, it is a near guarantee that the students are also disengaged. When teachers are authentically enthusiastic and engaged in the classroom, students most often will be, as well. Teachers should share with their students the various topics they are curious about, as well as the ways they challenge their own creative minds. When teachers model curiosity and creativity, it encourages students to do the same. Working together, teachers and students can together ask "Why?" and "Why not?" about the world around them.

Teachers also need to exercise a healthy Spirit of Adventure. More than 1 in 10 teachers (11%) are afraid to try something if they think they might fail. Teachers must be willing to try new things and take on new challenges within the school community. While the stakes may be high, the benefits are well worth the risk. As teachers venture into new territory and take healthy risks, colleagues and administrators must provide support that allows everyone to learn from successes and failures. Both will happen. These are not only learning opportunities for the teachers themselves but they provide another meaningful model for students.

TEACHER VOICE

It is up to me to make the classroom an exciting place for students and myself. Students are greeted daily with the title of "Scientist," and assessments are called "Science Parties." Students have really run with this, bringing cookies and showing up before school to decorate for Science Parties. I dress up as "Science Claus" before Christmas Break and assignments become "special gifts" from me. Cheesy science songs that relate to topics of study are played frequently. Smiles and laughter are exchanged when I catch students singing along while completing a lab or mouthing the words to a song to help them recall information on an assessment. These nuances have built positive bonds with students that payoff significantly.

Travis Lande
Junior High Science Teacher
12 Years Teaching Experience
Ballou Junior High
Puyallup School District
Puyallup, Washington

DEFINING A SENSE OF PURPOSE

Teachers, by nature and profession, want to make a difference. Yet in this era of deliverables, accountability, and real-time data, teachers are much more likely to be inundated with feedback about the ways they did *not* make a difference. To develop a sense of purpose, teachers need to be clear as to how they *are* making a difference. They need genuine leadership opportunities where they can make decisions and take responsibility for their choices, as well as the opportunity to set personal goals and work with confidence to achieve them.

53% of teachers report having a voice in decision making at school.

Teachers have incredible perspectives and a wealth of knowledge to contribute to committees and leadership teams; their input can enhance the discourse about school-related decisions on nearly any topic. Teachers should be provided with meaningful leadership roles, opportunities to share in the responsibility for the school community, and autonomy in curriculum development and instructional strategies. Teachers should be leaders in conversations about formative assessments and rubric development. They should be invited to pilot new materials and encouraged to provide feedback for critical curricular decisions. Too often, the latest materials "guaranteed" to close the achievement gap are purchased and implemented in ways that teachers, had they been asked, could have forewarned would be unsuccessful. Teachers must be given authentic opportunities to play a central role in decision making that directly influences the teaching and learning environment. Teachers are charged with the greatest responsibility a school has—the students—it only makes sense that they have input in schoolwide decisions that ultimately affect teachers, students, and learning.

It is important to endorse teachers leading from their current role. Traditionally, teachers' desires to lead and take action have been confused with the desire to take on a new position with a different title and job description. There is an inaccurate belief that leadership and teaching are mutually exclusive. A brilliant and talented heart surgeon would not be told, "Wow! You are such a skillful heart surgeon! Why don't you become a hospital administrator? Or why don't you take charge of the hospital pharmacy? You are such a talented surgeon; therefore, we think that you should do something else." This surgeon would instead be encouraged to continue his or her practice, continue refining surgical practices, share techniques and strategies with colleagues, and perhaps teach and practice at a medical research hospital where others could learn from such an expert.

In "The Many Faces of Leadership," Charlotte Danielson (2007) sums up the damage that can result from a failure to provide valid opportunities for teachers to lead:

> *Teaching is a flat profession.* In most professions, as the practitioner gains experience, he or she has the opportunity to exercise greater responsibility and assume more significant challenges. This is not true of teaching. The 20-year veteran's responsibilities are essentially the same as those of the newly licensed novice. In many settings, the only way for a teacher to extend his or her influence is to become an administrator. Many teachers recognize that this is not the right avenue for them. The job of an administrator entails work that does not interest them, but they still have the urge to exercise wider influence in their schools and in the profession. This desire for greater responsibility, if left unfulfilled, can lead to frustration and even cynicism. (p. 14)

We cringe when we hear, "You could be so much more than a teacher!" Increasingly, our master teachers are told they should become school administrators or district staff members, as if these positions and titles are somehow more esteemed or valued than their role in the classroom. There is an automatic assumption made that the skill set of a master teacher would inherently make one an excellent assistant principal or assessment evaluator. Certainly, there is overlap in the skills required for each and value in various positions at all levels. But changing roles completely is not the answer to fostering leadership skills in teachers. Master teachers must be valued for increasing expertise *within their roles*, such as the achievement of National Board Certification. Teachers must be provided meaningful avenues for leading *while still teaching*—opportunities to be deeply involved in decision making and the responsibility associated with related action plans. This will develop a true sense of purpose among teachers.

*69% of teachers say they are excited about their
future career in education.*

Affording teachers the opportunity for professional growth within their role fosters excitement about their future in education. This allows them to continue working directly with students—the reason they entered education it the first place! "Moving up" in the education world is different than your traditional corporate ladder, or at least it should be. One does not necessarily have to be on a higher rung to have more influence. Done correctly, staying in the classroom could have more of a direct impact on students' lives than securing a position further up the perceived ladder of advancement. *And* it allows teachers to maintain their enjoyment and excitement of working with students. The key is for teachers to be included in the decision making that occurs at higher levels while allowing them to continue their valued role in the classroom. Collaboration should occur across all levels in education, with teachers working alongside principals and district leaders. If teachers steady themselves on the teaching rung as valued professionals directly responsible for the learning experience of students and are invited by those in administrative positions to share their voice and assume leadership roles within their schools, their sphere of influence will broaden. This will allow teachers to stay true to their purpose—to make a difference in the lives of students and their futures; indeed, to make a difference in the world—*and* have an influence in education beyond their classroom walls.

As Andy Hargreaves and Michael Fullan (2012) write in *Professional Capital: Transforming Teaching in Every School*, it is imperative that we move from a country in which the voices of teachers have become increasingly muted to seeing the capacity of our teachers "as nation builders . . . [able] to yield high returns in prosperity, social cohesion, and social justice" (p. 185). It is time to begin anew and honor the importance of teacher voice and rethink leadership opportunities in the education profession. Teachers can effectively lead from the very role they are in—becoming innovative trailblazers who continually improve their profession and the world—if only given the chance.

*79% of teachers see themselves as a leader, yet only 61% report
that their colleagues see them as a leader.*

The following two conditions serve to foster Purpose: Leadership and Responsibility and Confidence to Take Action.

To help teachers become true leaders, and define their own sense of purpose, meaningful opportunities to exercise Leadership and Responsibility must exist. It is important to state that this does *not* mean arbitrarily assigning teachers additional duties for tasks that need to be accomplished. Teachers and administrators should work together to uncover the interests and strengths of each individual and identify opportunities for leadership that prove to be a match. Leadership opportunities should be distributed throughout the entire staff; *every* teacher should have the genuine opportunity to learn and grow as a leader. Teachers must be ready to assume the responsibility that comes with leadership roles, and the support from colleagues and administrators in this endeavor is paramount. A shared sense of accountability for the school community enhances the sense of purpose for all involved.

Teachers must develop their own Confidence to Take Action, believing in themselves and being prepared to use their voice in leadership roles when opportunities are at hand. Exercising teacher voice to communicate and share ideas with others is an excellent start, but the rubber really meets the road when conversation and ideas turn to action. Teachers must seize opportunities to step up, get involved, and live out a sense of purpose by using their voice to take action and make a difference! There is no better time to start than today!

TEACHER VOICE

Who will lead Aspirations in our school? Who will staff and students follow? My assistant principal answered this when he approached me about leading the high school student Aspirations team. It was a turning point in my teaching career, as it became clear that he valued me enough to ask me to be the leader. After over 20 years in the classroom, Aspirations has changed how I listen to students and has significantly impacted *how* we approach change at our school to make things better.

Kurt Klingler
7-12 Technology Teacher
26 Years Teaching Experience
Ada High School
Ada, Ohio

As long as there have been teachers, there has been teacher voice. Certainly teacher voice has not been silent over the years. However, teacher voice is an underutilized resource in efforts to improve the teaching and learning environment. Schools have yet to put in place a system that will not only guarantee teacher voice but embrace it as an accepted, integral part of the regular operations of schools.

Make no mistake; tapping into and maximizing this resource is not a quick-fix process! There will be challenges throughout the journey, for both teachers and on the organizational side. But the journey will be worth the effort when the ethos of schools reflects teachers with a true sense of self-worth, who are highly engaged in the school and professional learning, and who have a clear purpose as educators.

Teachers have a great deal to say, and it is of vital importance that schools, and the educational community at large, listen to, learn from, *and lead with* them. Now is the time for teacher voice to be realized as an active agent in school change. In fact, it is way overdue.

TEACHER VOICE MAKING A DIFFERENCE

There are indeed tremendous and ever-changing challenges facing today's teachers, a fact not to be diminished. Requirements and expectations continuously shift, often in relatively short periods of time, and with less than stellar support. With that in mind, it is important to have a clear picture of what effective incorporation of teacher voice looks like; so all stakeholders can begin the journey with a shared vision.

Purposeful teacher voice exists when teachers and the organization are engaged and show genuine interest in establishing a strong working relationship built on trust and responsibility. Teachers are eager and willing to be involved and take responsibility in the school community. Rather than bemoaning the challenges, the majority of conversation is focused on generating solutions. The organization recognizes, celebrates, and actively seeks out teacher voice. In the ideal system, teacher voice becomes an *essential* part of the organizational structure and function. It becomes part of the day-to-day operations. Administrators and teachers share ownership for the teaching and learning environment and the well-being of every individual within the school. Effective use of voice includes active listening by both the teachers and the organization, allowing for a rich teaching and learning environment.

Once teacher voice becomes part of the fabric of a system, it will be difficult to imagine how things could have ever operated any differently. The idea of an organization in which teachers did not have a powerful and productive voice will be simply preposterous.

Teachers and administrators need to start the journey and allow time to travel along the pathway to meaningful teacher voice. Effective change will not occur overnight, but each step toward teacher voice is one in the right direction.

The Guiding Principles can be used as road map along the pathway to teacher voice to help guide school improvement efforts. This allows individuals and organizations to identify their current location and determine a plan for moving forward. Each school's journey to effective teacher voice will be different, with their own starting point, pathway, and unique learning environment. There is no scripted implementation plan, and there is more than one way to reach desired outcomes. The pathway is not designed to provide step-by-step instructions. That would go against everything this book stands for! Instead, the pathway is a guide—a compass, as opposed to a road map; the Guiding Principles of self-worth, engagement, and purpose provide the scaffolding for bringing teacher voice to the forefront of change.

Individual teachers and school organizations have the potential to embrace teacher voice and create a culture that will allow it to thrive. When teachers are ready to exercise their voice and engage in the shared responsibilities of the school, and organizations simultaneously provide a context in which this can occur, then teacher voice will flourish.

It is well accepted that real cultural changes that last do not occur overnight. It has been argued that the most meaningful change in schools takes a minimum of three to five years. We are cognizant that the various pathways to teacher voice may include serious detours along the way. However, being somewhat impatient individuals, we would argue that the teachers and children sitting in our schools right now do not have three to five years to wait. We believe that the resolve and drive of any group of passionate educators is far more powerful than any pre-established timetable for change.

It will be a significant journey; but one well worth the effort, and one that must be expedited for the sake of every individual in our education system. While the most far-reaching change may not happen in short order, the changes made in the short term will still have an immediate impact on teachers and the students they serve and set the tone for the longer journey. Just remember: You have to share the steering wheel! This is not a solo trip.

Action Steps to Embrace Teacher Voice

- **Start the year off with a bang!** Staff retreats (developed with teacher input, of course!) at the beginning of the school year help build relationships and set a collegial tone for the year. Plan time for teachers to work with one another on projects driven by their interests and centered around activities that will directly impact students.

- **Provide training on effective communication skills.** It is often presumed that teachers are naturally great communicators, but that is not always the case. Working on communication skills should be a regular part of staff development opportunities.

- **Be proactive and positive.** Welcome all ideas—both mainstream and outside-the-box thinking. Use both to fuel change, staying focused on solution-oriented approaches. Dialogue should include responses to the question "How can we make a positive change to address this?"

- **Celebrate successes frequently.** Acknowledge quality work and progress on a regular basis, not just at the end of the school year. Teachers should share their best practices at staff meetings, online, at regional and national professional meetings, and/or through journal writings and op-eds. The key is to let people know (within the school and the community) how impressive teachers are and how their voices are making a positive difference.

- **Create a culture of respect and openness.** Model honesty and respect, and expect it from colleagues. Cultivate an atmosphere that allows for collegial dissent, respect for alternate points of view, and the opportunity to learn from differing opinions. To be really committed to listening, one needs to be prepared to learn with an open mind.

- **Facilitate teachers teaching teachers.** Schedule monthly "Learn Something New" sessions centered on teachers' areas of expertise. Teachers can teach their colleagues about a wide variety of topics determined by need and interest.

- **Identify leadership roles.** Teachers, alongside the administration, need to brainstorm areas of school life in which they can and should have leadership roles. Develop implementation steps, ways to measure progress, and get started!

Teacher Reflections

1. How do you currently exercise your voice in meaningful and productive ways? What are two concrete ways you can improve in this area?

2. How do you know if your voice is valued at school? How is your voice reflected in the culture, policies, and practices of your school?

3. Who are your professional heroes? Why?

4. What opportunities can your school provide to engage you in leadership responsibilities that match your interests and strengths?

CHAPTER 4

Expression of Teacher Voice

When using your voice, exercise your ears as much as your mouth.

Ask nearly any teacher in a faculty room or at a weekend barbecue what they think about the Common Core, standardized tests, or new curriculum requirements and they will likely have plenty to say! Teachers' comments, like most humans, will often focus on current challenges with what can be interpreted as a negative tone. Chip and Dan Heath (2010) analyzed various studies on the concept of "bad is stronger than good." They were actually looking for exceptions to this phenomenon but were unable to find any examples of good being consistently stronger than bad. One study they reference analyzed the use of 558 emotion words and found that 62% were negative and only 32% were positive. Other studies have shown that people spend longer looking at pictures of bad events than good and consistently pay closer attention when told bad things about people. The pull to talk about the bad is apparently natural, but we are advocating for greater balance in conversations about education. Conversations that include plenty of good!

Step 1 to a more balanced conversation about schools is to acknowledge the human tendency to focus on the negative. Step 2 is making thoughtful, deliberate efforts to increase positive conversations about education. Step 3 is to keep step one in mind and repeat step two over and over again!

Step 1: Recognize human tendency to focus on the negative.

Step 2: Make thoughtful, deliberate efforts to increase positive conversations about education.

Step 3: Keep step one in mind and repeat step two over and over again! ■

BALANCED CONVERSATION

When falling prey to the natural gravitation toward the negative, teachers can get a bad rap and be perceived as perpetually complaining about low pay, large class sizes, and the growing list of demands and pressures for students to achieve on questionable measures. There are indeed many aspects of the teaching profession that are in need of improvement. However, getting stuck in a quagmire of admiring problems does not contribute to forward progress. Educators frequently express their desire to be viewed more favorably and professionally by the public. We fully support this! We are simultaneously aware that teachers must reflect on their own current mindset and expression of teacher voice, and they must be mindful of their impact within and around the school community. Teacher voice is powerful and can make an incredibly positive difference, but only if it is consciously utilized with the good in mind!

■ ■ ■ BALANCED CONVERSATION IN ACTION

One of my (LL) professional mentors, Dr. Marybeth Flachbart, frequently practiced a strategy with teams to combat the "bad is stronger than good" phenomenon. When a problem was presented, she would provide teams with a set amount of time to "admire the problem," allowing individuals to vent and discuss various aspects of the challenge. At what always seemed to be the perfect time, Dr. Flachbart would stop the conversation and declare that the "admiring the problem" time had expired. The conversation would then turn to seeking solutions and imagining what the situation would look like once the problem had been effectively addressed. ■

When conversations about schools are primarily focused on the challenges, a negative public perception of schools develops. More balanced conversations, including examples of what is going well in schools, have the power to positively impact the way schools are viewed and supported. We are not suggesting that current issues should be ignored or even sugarcoated. Rather, we are advocating for teachers to engage in balanced conversations. Teachers need to share positive things happening in schools, while also addressing aspects in need of improvement—approaching both in a professional and meaningful way. There is a great deal to be learned from both the good and the bad, as long as conversations remain productive and solutions oriented, with the ultimate goal being an improved learning experience for students and teachers. Balanced conversations should permeate the dialogue within a school and flow into discussions about education beyond the walls of the building, both in the surrounding geographical community and in the larger virtual community.

BRIGHT SPOTS

The Heath brothers write about the power of focusing on "bright spots" as one way to address human default toward the negative. "To pursue bright spots is to ask the

■■■ BRIGHT SPOTS RESOURCE

For more information on bright spots, including a clever video that provides a conceptual overview, check out:

Dan Heath: How to Find Bright Spots

https://www.youtube.com/watch?v=zbLNOS7MxFc ■

TEACHER VOICE

I am a proud public school teacher. I am proud to teach students from all walks of life. I am proud of the democratic ideal of improving a community through education. I am also a proud parent of public school students. I use my voice in my community to express that pride. I back up my words with my actions. I attend school events, I send money, I volunteer, and I work hard. I praise the schools of which I am a part, whether as a teacher or as parent. Community schools thrive on positive voices in their communities.

Gay Buckland-Murray
French Teacher
23 Years Teaching Experience
Woodside High School
Sequoia Union High School District
Redwood City, California

question, 'What's working, and how can we do more of it?' Sounds simple, right? Yet, in the real world, this obvious question is rarely asked. Instead, the question raised is typically problem centered: 'What's broken, and how do we fix it?'" (2010, p. 45). We believe that both questions should be asked; the two serve to complement one another in a balanced approach to conversations about education.

EFFECTIVE COMMUNICATION

48% of teachers report that they communicate effectively in their school.

Whether about the good or the challenges in schools, there is important work to be done to improve the effectiveness of communication itself among teachers. It is a false assumption that teachers are inherently effective communicators. One can be quite effective talking to people shorter than themselves (students of course) yet feel like a fish out of water engaging in conversations with adults. (We thought you might be missing the fishing references!) The skill set necessary to successfully communicate with students is not one and the same as the skills needed to effectively communicate with colleagues and school leaders.

TEACHER VOICE

When I was a beginning teacher, it seemed as if my voice was on mute. I thought I had great ideas, but according to the administrator and a few veteran teachers, I was not experienced enough to be heard. Now, as a veteran teacher, I have observed teachers' voices not being heard specifically because their students are not achieving academic success, their attitudes are not professional, or their approach does not "set the stage" for being heard. To overcome these barriers, teachers must first know that we all have a voice, whether novice or experienced. Second, you have to know your audience and your purpose. Third, your actions speak louder than words, so be the example. Last, it is so important to know that it is not what you say, it is how you say it.

Danielle Hickerson, EdD
Cobb County School District
Marietta, Georgia

Countless books have been written on the topic of effective communication, and many are worthy of recommendation. There is one in particular that we believe should be required reading for every educator: Jim Knight's book *Better Conversations: Coaching Ourselves and Each Other to Be More Credible, Caring, and Connected.* Knight masterfully synthesizes the literature on communication and also shares insights from his own research and wealth of knowledge. He writes, "When trust, respect, and clear communication are cultural norms, teachers are more comfortable sharing ideas and learning from each other. Better conversations will improve collaboration, team meetings, professional learning communities, and other conversations about teaching and learning. Better conversations also lead to fewer hard feelings and more listening, respect, kindness, and candor" (2016, p. 3). Knight's book is a gold mine of practical strategies for improving communication skills and developing better conversation habits (see box, Jim Knight's Better Conversation Habits). Knight's work and publications have had a profound impact on both of our lives and the way we communicate professionally and personally. As a token of our gratitude, we may just have to invite him to join our next fishing adventure!

■■■ JIM KNIGHT'S BETTER CONVERSATION HABITS

1. Demonstrating Empathy

2. Listening With Empathy

3. Fostering Dialogue

4. Asking Better Questions

5. Making Emotional Connections

6. Being a Witness to the Good

7. Finding Common Ground

8. Controlling Toxic Emotions

9. Redirecting Toxic Conversations

10. Building Trust

To further explore how to develop these habits, read *Better Conversations: Coaching Ourselves and Each Other to Be More Credible, Caring, and Connected* (Knight, 2016). ■

EXPRESSION OF TEACHER VOICE LINKED TO THE GUIDING PRINCIPLES

The way teachers express their voice is significantly impacted by their belief regarding the value of their voice. All teachers *have* a voice; each has individual thoughts and opinions. However, many teachers *feel* a lack of support in their school systems when it comes to actually exercising their voice. "All human beings want their voices to matter. We like giving our opinions and offering ideas. We want to be the subject of our activities, not the objects of someone else's. We want to be active agents, not just passive spectators" (Quaglia & Corso, 2014, p. 2). Teachers' beliefs regarding the value of their voice directly impact the way their voice is used in schools.

The voice of every teacher *will be* exercised within the school and community. It is important to recognize various ways in which voice tends to play out in a school system. Part of that process is discovering how to best listen and how to collectively cultivate voice that is valued and effective for every member of the school system. There are countless ways that voice can be expressed; we offer a few examples for consideration. These examples are connected to the 3 Guiding Principles previously discussed: Self-Worth, Engagement, and Purpose. Within each example is an opportunity to make forward progress on the pathway to teacher voice, embedding the Guiding Principles into the ethos of the school along the way.

FROM DOMINANCE TO BALANCE (SELF-WORTH)

Voices that roll out with a domineering tone are often heard from individuals who are incredibly passionate about teaching and believe they are advocating in the best interest of the school. While they are often well intended, they unintentionally alienate others and can be viewed as overwhelming and overbearing. These voices are so audibly dominant that little space is left for others to contribute to the conversation.

Many principals report spending a significant amount of time working with the loud minority and wondering what the many silent voices might have to say. It can be easy to assume that the majority of teachers are in agreement with the voices that are the loudest and most frequent. This, however, may not be the case. The remainder of the teaching staff is often desperately waiting for leadership to address the loud minority and provide space for other voices to be heard. If space is not made for all voices to be heard, the school culture can become toxic.

It is important to recognize that this does not meet shutting down loud voices or dismissing alternative perspectives. There are often significant lessons to be learned from dissenting opinions; they have considered ideas from different angles that can benefit a balanced conversation. However, a loud contingent that does not provide space for the input of others should not be rewarded for their domineering voices by capturing the majority of time and attention from leadership. Principals can create balance by listening to the perspectives of the loud voices while also providing space for all members of the school community to exercise their voice.

Ideally, individuals that may be dominating conversation would engage in self-reflection and monitor themselves when their voice is becoming too domineering. One of the best ways strong, vocal teachers can contribute to the school community is to represent the ideas of others in addition to their own perspectives. With the right disposition and approach, vocal teachers can also help colleagues who are less comfortable with group conversations to develop the confidence to express their own voices.

IN ACTION: BALANCING THE CONVERSATION

At the conclusion of yet another staff meeting dominated by one teacher, the principal knew she needed to address the behavior. She could see the other teachers shutting down, holding back eye rolls, and resentment growing for the lack of balance in staff discussions.

The principal began the next meeting by thanking the teacher for being so passionate and concerned about the wellbeing of the school. She validated the value of the input and shared how it informed the possible solutions for the issue at hand. She reminded all teachers of the guidelines for collaboration that had been agreed upon at the start of the year, including the staff's commitment to provide time and space for all voices to be heard. She acknowledged that sometimes there is not enough time for everyone to be heard and committed to keeping an eye on the clock and balancing "floor time." She also introduced an overtime box—a place where teachers could submit additional thoughts and ideas that they did not have time to share during the meeting. They were also invited to send her an e-mail with "overtime" in the subject line. In this effort to preserve the culture they had worked so hard to build, the principal also promised to reply to any "overtime" entries within 48 hours. She modeled a commitment to honoring *all* voices in the school community. ∎

TEACHER VOICE

When I think of an individual's voice that I sit up and listen to every time I hear it, it is a voice of compassion, consideration, thoughtfulness, and intelligence. It is a voice emanating from one person's mouth, yet capable of expressing the views of many. I respect voices like these because they speak for people like me. These voices know me and my thoughts. I am shy, or maybe I just don't like to speak in front of a group of my peers, so this kind voice gets to know me and likes my ideas and helps me share thoughts that might otherwise never come out.

Melissa Eagney
1st Grade Teacher
Spruce Creek Elementary
Volusia County Schools
Port Orange, Florida

All teachers have unique skills and talents behind their perspectives, and all can make valuable contributions to collegial conversations. It is the job of the entire school community to value, pursue, foster, and capitalize on all this—for *every* individual within the system.

73% of teachers believe they are valued
for their unique skills and talents.

It is critical that all input is honored—positive, negative, supportive, and challenging. All ideas must be shared and listened to with respect, particularly when discord is involved, followed by a collective movement into solution-oriented conversations.

When self-regulation and balance are absent, action must be taken by colleagues and leadership to bring all voices back into the conversation; the health of the school culture depends on it! When traveling along the voice pathway from dominance to balance, strive to engage all voices in collaboration and address issues from a solution-based approach. When dialogue focuses on solutions, the conversation shifts from complaining to empowering; this energizes educators within a collegial learning environment and motives them to share their voice and make a difference. Balanced conversations—in voice and perspectives—is the goal. *Every* teacher should feel accepted and valued for their unique perspectives and contributions to the learning community.

FROM DORMANCY TO ENGAGEMENT (ENGAGEMENT)

Completely silent voices can be just as detrimental to the health of a school system as dominant voices. Teachers may choose not to exercise their voice for a variety of reasons. Some are silent out of discomfort for sharing in large groups. Others fear the nature of responses from colleagues and administration. Some have just given up trying to be heard over the loud, constant voices. It is also possible that some simply do not want a voice. They are happy just showing up and doing the minimal amount required to skate through each day. (We suggest that it might be time for those individuals to find a new profession!)

Silence can also be a result of teachers becoming so frustrated with the school environment that they shut down. They simply refuse to engage. It would be a mistake to assume that silence equates to agreement. Silence reflects lack of engagement, not lack of opinion. It is not that these teachers do not have ideas to share; they have unfortunately come to believe it is not worth the effort.

A variety of approaches are needed to address the various causes of voice dormancy. The frustrated, silent-because-it-is-not-worth-it voices have the potential to cause havoc once released from their bottled-up state. This is not entirely a bad thing; there is a silver lining. As mentioned previously, a great deal can be learned from dissonant voices. The same could be true for voices that feel drowned out by others.

Whether the voices are in harmony or discord, teacher voice must be brought out into the open. If only expressed behind closed doors, these voices can indeed be harmful to a school culture. To preempt this, create an environment where voices of agreement and dissenting opinions are valued and safe to express. To establish this type of openness, consider assigning a teacher to play devil's advocate on a rotating basis during staff meetings, similar to how teachers assign pro and con sides for student debates. This demonstrates an interest in exploring all sides of an issue, provides a comfortable space for teachers to express opinions in a healthy context, and models respectful consideration of diverse opinions.

In addition to providing a safe environment for expressing a variety of perspectives in large groups, seek out individuals who have been unintentionally silenced, or who elect to disengage in large groups due to general discomfort or fear of others' responses. The goal is to restore their voices and engage them in the school community. Every voice matters. Regardless of the position or title, all individuals should know that their contributions to the school really matter. "When you make someone feel valuable, you're telling the person, 'You have a reason for being here. You have a reason for getting out of bed every morning and doing everything you do. You have a reason for being a part of this family, this company, this world. It makes a difference that you are here.' When you make people feel important, you give them a gift that is beyond price" (Goulston, 2010, p. 64).

It may sound funny, but it is not enough when teachers are admired and valued by others. If those thoughts remain internal, then the teachers will never know! It is imperative that *the teachers know* their contributions are valued by others. The appreciation must be overt. There should be absolutely no uncertainty in teachers' minds that the engagement of their voice is an integral part of creating an engaging learning environment for all.

> *Only 56% of teachers claim they are recognized when they try their best, while 19% of teachers say they have never been recognized for anything positive at school.*

When teachers believe their voice is valued, they become more engaged and active in their school. Odds analysis studies within our research on teacher voice show

- Teachers who are comfortable expressing their honest opinions and concerns are four times more likely to be excited about their future career in education.

- When teachers have voice, they are three times more likely to value setting goals and work hard to reach those goals.

- When teachers have a voice in decision making, they are four times more likely to believe they can make a difference. They are also three times more likely to encourage students to be leaders and make decisions!

(QISA & TVAIC, 2015)

TEACHER VOICE

There are a few first and second year teachers within my school. Often I have noticed in a meeting they look around as if they have a comment or idea when a question is posed to the entire group or staff. Usually they do not respond within the whole group. During a particular meeting, I was seated next to a first year teacher and she shared a great idea with me. I said, "You should share that with the staff. It is a great idea!" She declined, so I asked her would it be alright if I shared her idea for her with the staff. Once I shared her idea by starting with "I just heard a great idea from Sara (not real name). . . . " She loved the feedback and smiles she received from her idea. It was a moment that made her feel that she had really valuable information, even as a first year teacher, to help others.

Tamla Chambless
3rd Grade Teacher
10 Years Teaching Experience
Clarkdale Elementary School
Cobb County School District
Marietta, Georgia

As discussed in Chapter 3, excellent teachers who are highly engaged are often channeled into administrative roles. It is assumed to be the next logical step to keep them interested in the profession. But we must disregard the typical corporate ladder in education and consider other possibilities for teachers to engage in leadership while remaining in the classroom.

The authors of *Teacherpreneurs: Innovative Teachers Who Lead but Don't Leave*, cite a recent MetLife study, which found that 84% of teachers are not interested in becoming a principal. Twenty-three percent did, however, report being interested in serving in some kind of teacher-leader role. This hybrid space is being filled by what they call the "teacherpreneur—a classroom expert who still teaches while finding time, space, and (ideally) much-deserved reward for spreading both sound pedagogical practices and policy ideas" (Berry, Byrd, & Weider, 2013, p. xvii). What an innovative concept: passionate teachers who remain in the classroom and yet are provided with meaningful opportunities to take on hybrid leadership roles. Imagine how teacher voice would be amplified if we embraced this concept of *teacherpreneurs* and unleashed the innovative, creative side of our teaching force, allowing them to apply their skills beyond the walls of their classroom.

Teach to Lead, a partnership between the U.S. Department of Education, the National Board, and the Association of Supervision and Curriculum Development (ASCD), is an example of a program designed to keep great teachers in the classroom, while giving them meaningful opportunities to lead. A core belief of Teach to Lead is that "expanded educator voice inside of education will make policies smarter and implementation smoother" (Fennell, 2016). The Center for Teaching Quality and their Teacher Leaders Network, Teach Plus, the NEA Teacher Leadership Initiative, and the VIVA Project are a few additional examples of organizations working to increase teacher leadership and voice within the classroom and beyond.

99% of teachers believe learning can be fun and that
they enjoy learning new things, yet only 69% of teachers
are encouraged to be creative at school.

While it might require great effort, every single teacher voice must be meaningfully engaged, not only for the professional and personal health of individuals but also for the overall well-being of the school community. Jim Knight states that "professional learning needs to value the opinions of all participants, not just those of the change leader. In fact, learning is significantly limited unless everyone's voice is encouraged and heard" (2011, p. 34). When all voices are encouraged and heard, engagement grows with limitless possibilities for systemwide impact. When teachers feel authentically valued, they are much more likely to move from dormancy to engagement. From there, the options are plentiful.

FROM TALK TO ACTION (PURPOSE)

Sometimes individuals who talk the most actually say very little. This expression of voice is like wandering through the desert with no destination in sight. It is difficult to interpret the message trying to be communicated, and there seems to be little or no action linked to the syllables. Those who struggle with this phenomenon would do well to take some advice from Elvis Presley's famous lyric, "a little less conversation, a little more action!"

Those stuck in the talking trap wish to have a powerful voice, but over time, others eventually stop listening. Sometimes these over-talkers are viewed as pests or perpetual complainers. The flip side of that coin is that these teachers have great potential. With guidance on how to appropriately exercise their voice and the development of strong communication skills, these individuals can become an incredible asset within a culture that values and acts on teacher voice. The goal is to channel the eager voices into productive action.

William Damon, a psychologist and researcher at Stanford University, defines purpose as an intention to accomplish something that is "meaningful to the self and consequential for the world beyond the self" (2008, p. 33). Those that are in a cycle of too much talk and too little action not only alienate others but eventually fizzle out and become disengaged themselves when nothing of substance is achieved. While they may be able to articulate their vision and purpose,

"I am starting to think that my colleagues are intentionally avoiding me," a frustrated teacher expressed to an instructional coach. "At every single grade level meeting this year, I have told the team that we *have* to find a new approach for teaching math, but it seems like no one is listening. One teacher even nodded off while I was talking at our last collaboration meeting!"

The coach paused and then replied, "I hear that you have raised this issue many times. What solutions have you offered? Have you suggested any ideas or strategies on how to improve the current approach?"

"No," replied the teacher. "I thought someone else would figure out what we actually have to *do*." ■

they never experience the benefits of a sense of accomplishment or concrete realization of the defined purpose.

How do we help over-talkers harness their thinking, clearly articulate their thoughts, and take action? As communication skills are refined, goal setting and action plans should be put into place. With clearly defined goals established to support a motivating purpose and concrete steps to achieve these goals outlined, individuals will gain the confidence to take action.

Confidence to take action is the extent to which teachers believe in themselves and their ability to really make a difference. We characterize confidence to take action "by a positive and healthy outlook on life and by looking inward rather than outward for motivation and approval" (Quaglia & Corso, 2014, p. 131). As progress is made toward achieving established goals, a true sense of accomplishment will grow. Teachers will see firsthand the concrete ways in which their ideas can be realized. This, in turn, expands one's motivation to continue turning talk into action, *with purpose*.

TEACHER VOICE: FROM LAME TO FAME

	FROM LAME . . .	TO FAME!
Self-Worth	Paula, an incredibly passionate teacher, takes the lead on an effort to add several new AP courses to the course offerings. Paula does an incredible amount of preparation and worries that if everything is not done according to her well-constructed plan, the effort might fail. Considering all that needs to	Paula provides a brief overview of a draft plan for adding new AP course offerings and then has small groups generate questions, concerns, and possibilities to consider. Adding courses impacts the schedule and school environment for everyone, and it is important to Paula that all voices are included in the process.

	be done in a short period of time, Paula dominates the staff meeting outlining her plan but is sure to include others by giving them assigned tasks.	
Engagement	The science department is talking about applying for a grant. Alex has a unique idea for how they can measure results, but he keeps his thoughts to himself. What if his colleagues think his idea is stupid? There are plenty of other people who contribute during meetings, and sharing his idea just is not worth the risk. It is much easier to sit back silently.	As a first step to exercising his voice with his colleagues, Alex approaches the chair of the science department after the meeting and shares his idea for the grant application. They engage in productive dialogue and the chair asks Alex if he would be willing to share the idea with the whole department at their next meeting.
Purpose	For months, Tiffany has been sharing her frustration about the flat-lined reading scores at the team collaboration meetings. She sounds and feels a bit like a broken record, saying over and over how ineffective the intervention program is, that it is a waste of time, and it lacks results.	After trying a few different tweaks to the reading intervention program, Tiffany proposes the team try a new strategy that is generating improved results with some of her students. She asks her team to help further refine the strategy with the goal of improved results for all their students.

EFFECTIVE EXPRESSION OF TEACHER VOICE

We hope everyone reading this book is interested in moving from lame to fame conversations! Based on countless conversations of our own, observations, and lessons learned from our own failures and successes, we offer the following strategies for effectively expressing teacher voice:

1. **Be Bold and Brave.** Every teacher has a responsibility to positively contribute to the school community. Student success depends on what happens within the walls of the entire school, not just individual classrooms. Teachers enter the profession with varying comfort levels for communicating with colleagues. For some, being bold and brave will mean speaking up, even when it feels like a risky thing to do. It is important for these individuals to remember that all ideas make an impact. Even those that end up in the discard pile can serve to inform and advance the thought process. For others, being bold and brave will mean intentionally making space for the voices of others. This can mean embracing an idea far different from your own and being open to doing things differently. Whether stepping up, or stepping back, do so boldly and bravely!

2. **Exemplify Professionalism.** Teaching staff can sometimes feel like a second family. This can be a good thing or a very challenging thing! Yes, it is critical to know the hopes and dreams of colleagues and develop strong working relationships with one another. It is equally essential that professionalism guides all teacher conversation, especially when difficulties arise. Misplaced sarcasm and passive aggressiveness are common enemies of professionalism. When times get tough and conversations get heated, it is important to take a deep breath and remember that colleagues are not actually siblings to verbally spar with! Ensure that all conversations, public and private, exemplify professionalism. The power of teacher voice, individually and collectively, depends on the ability to use that voice professionally . . . *all* the time.

3. **Remain Solution Oriented.** Talking about and admiring problems is easier than the effort it takes to solve a problem. However, circling a challenge with never ending negativity not only perpetuates the problem but also erodes a positive school culture. Voices with the greatest positive impact are those that embrace a solution-oriented mindset. For every challenge that is voiced, ideas should be offered about how to tackle the problem. This comes naturally to some and will require a serious retraining of the brain for others. Keep in mind that there are typically multiple approaches to solving a problem. The best solutions are often a blend of multiple ideas.

4. **Remember to Listen, Learn, and Lead.** This circles back to the School Voice Model at the heart of our work. Always remember the astounding power of truly listening: Listening with an authentic intent to learn from the voices of others and then take action collaboratively and lead based upon what you learned.

■ ■ ■ EFFECTIVE EXPRESSION OF TEACHER VOICE STRATEGIES

1. Be Bold and Brave.
2. Exemplify Professionalism.
3. Remain Solution Oriented.
4. Remember to Listen, Learn, and Lead. ■

VOICE WITH BALANCE, ENGAGEMENT, AND ACTION

The epitome of teacher voice in a school, what we all should be striving for, is a balanced expression of teacher voice that leads to engagement and action. This manifestation of voice is thoughtful, honest, and considerate of others. It is a confident voice, but one that exercises self-restraint and frequently invites the voices of others to join the conversation. Teachers with a balanced, engaged, and action-oriented voice are highly skilled in the art of communication and are just as effective at listening as they are at speaking. Most importantly, the ideal voice is always focused on saying and doing what is best for students.

We can assign descriptors to various expressions of teacher voice to help us reflect on the ways voice is used and to provide common language for discussion. But what matters most is that every individual in a school system works toward creating a school culture that honors and incorporates every teacher voice, regardless of how it is expressed. All voices in a school community are worthy of being heard, both when individuals are at their best and when they are in the midst of struggle.

It has been written that, "Student voice is the instrument of change. We are at a point when we and our students must stand up and be heard or the educational policy mongers will continue to strip us of the basic purpose of education, which is to allow our students to dream, reach, and succeed" (Quaglia & Corso, 2014, p. 174). If student voice is the *instrument of change*, we propose that teacher voice can be the tool to *amplify the success* of improvement efforts. It is not possible for student voice to thrive if those responsible for the education of young people do not also have a voice. We dream of schools in which students and teachers *both* have voice; where they are not afraid to share their honest opinions and concerns, ask questions, and try new things; where they are learners, instructors, and advocates alongside one another and collaborating with one another; where they are afforded regular opportunities to listen, learn, and lead.

It is crucial for teacher and student voice to be heard in harmony—not in the sense that all ideas are the same and/or in sync, but in a way that reflects working together to create something beautiful that honors discord and seeks solutions that benefit all. In the case of education, we are striving for a learning environment that enriches the self-worth, engagement, and purpose for all involved. It is not that everyone is in perfect agreement, but the harmony of their goals, and mutual respect for their shared purpose, creates a perfect opportunity to amplify the success of students and teachers alike. Then all will thrive . . . and continue to drive school improvement efforts.

Action Steps to Improve Teacher Voice

- **Speak up, with balance.** Engage in conversations not only about the challenges in education but with solutions for identified issues. Balance conversations to include bright spots and to help shape a positive public narrative about education.

- **Seek to understand.** Engage in conversation with others with perspectives that differ from your own. Take time to consider what lies behind the frustrated, complaint-ridden voices. Determine what can be learned from their position and work toward solutions that reflect the perspectives of all.

- **Collaborate.** Set a tone of balanced conversations by establishing collaboration as a school norm. Value all voices in the school community with a focus on listening, learning, and leading.

- **Publically celebrate.** Be proactive. Seek out opportunities to celebrate schools and individual teachers publically. Build relationships with local media and invite them as partners in continually celebrating and improving local education.

- **Establish discussion leaders.** On a rotating basis, identify different teachers individually or in pairs to lead discussions at each staff meeting. This will not eliminate loud voices, but it will provide others the opportunity to be heard and valued on a regular basis.

- **Create hybrid leadership roles.** Provide time for teachers to work on district, state, and national committees around topics relevant to your school (this may include curriculum-specific topics, innovation strategies, or new pedagogies) while remaining a classroom instructor. This may require creativity to provide support for teachers to succeed in both the classroom and in leadership. Consider factors such as scheduling, providing stipends, and recognition for efforts that go above and beyond.

- **Provide a variety of opportunities for voice.** Faculty meetings should not be the only place where teachers can exercise their voice. Create other avenues for teachers to share their ideas such as focus groups, Google docs, newsletters, blogs, or an Edmodo group.

- **Identify projects with purpose.** With input from teachers, determine opportunities to address defined needs at the school. To establish clear and shared purpose, collaborate with teachers to outline specific goals and concrete ways they can be achieved.

- **Post teacher strengths.** All teachers can learn from the strengths and skills of other teachers, but the skill sets need to be celebrated and shared. Invite teachers to confidently share areas of strength and create a master list. If a teacher would like assistance with technology or classroom management, for example, they will know which colleagues to seek out for ideas and support.

Teacher Reflections

1. Are you currently engaged in any conversations that are overly negative? How might you seek greater balance in conversations about that particular topic?

2. Within the overall conversations of your school community, is your voice overengaged, underengaged, or just right? How will you find, or keep, that just right balance?

3. What opportunities exist in your school system for teachers to advance their professional goals and utilize their talents while remaining in the classroom?

4. Are you involved in a conversation that has yet to result in action? How might you support turning talk into action?

5. What communication structures exist that ensure that you, and all teachers, contribute to collegial conversations?

CHAPTER 5

Teacher Voice: Circle of Influence and Inspiration

Just like fingerprints, your voice is unique to you . . . use it wisely.

The voice of teachers has the ability to influence every member of the school community. That's powerful. We are not referring to powerful as in the manner of a ruler or authoritarian. We are talking about influential—about the opportunity that exists for teachers to impact progress in education within their community. The teacher voice we are advocating for is utilized for the benefit of everyone, ultimately leading to a better teaching and learning environment. From students to community members, teachers have the potential to either positively or negatively impact those around them. As referenced previously, teacher voice is about *listening* to others, *learning* from what is being said, and *leading* by taking action together. When used effectively, teachers listen at least as often as they speak, put more energy into learning than trying to convince others, and lead by taking action with the best interest of all concerned in mind. This chapter explores the impact teacher voice has on students, colleagues, administrative leaders, parents, and community members.

■■ ESSENTIAL UNDERSTANDING

When used effectively, teachers listen at least as often as they speak, put more energy into learning than trying to convince others, and lead by taking action with the best interest of all concerned in mind. ■

Teachers do not exist in isolation. Unfortunately, most schools are organized in a way that makes them feel as though they are secluded. Schools do not inherently promote collaboration and communication. The structure of classrooms, schedules driven by time rather than learning, and sporadic meetings between key players (administrators, teachers, and students) can significantly limit key aspects of fostering teacher voice. Quite frankly, it is a small miracle that there is as much communication going on as there is! While the structure of schools can provide a challenge for teachers, that just means teacher voice must be even more purposeful and driven by the desire to be understood and heard. As detailed earlier, teachers must be willing to accept the challenges of having a voice, and the organization must simultaneously be ready to provide conditions where teacher voice will be listened to and valued. This takes time and effort, but just like fishing, the potential is always there. Teachers should not be afraid to go ahead and be the first to cast a line.

Teachers have the ability to inspire, motivate, and raise the aspirations of the people they are in contact with every day. And yet teacher voice is one of the most underutilized resources we have in schools. We don't think teachers fully understand their own potential when it comes to influencing others and ultimately having an impact on the entire educational system. Teacher Voice: Actions and Related Outcomes illustrates the actions teachers can take using their voices, along with related outcomes for key members of the school community.

TEACHER VOICE: ACTIONS AND RELATED OUTCOMES

TEACHER ACTIONS	OUTCOMES
Inspire Students	Engaged Learners
Encourage Colleagues	Motivated Teachers
Influence Leadership	Trusted Relationships
Guide Parents	Involved Families
Inform Community	Supportive Partnerships

STUDENTS

Students are predominantly viewed as the recipients of all that schools have to offer. Rather than one-way participation, students need to be considered partners in the learning process—indeed, in all aspects of school. As consumers of a major airline, we have the option to respond to surveys, or select "Contact Us" to submit a suggestion (or complaint!). But when we have something to say, how much do they really listen? How authentically is the feedback considered? How wholeheartedly would the feedback be considered if an owner of the company were the one to submit the feedback? The airline certainly would listen to the owner! The point is that students should be *partners in* their education and *part of* education reform. Do we listen to their feedback as if they were the owner of the company? They have first-hand experience in schools, they know what works and does not work for them as learners, and they are the very people schools were designed to support! It only makes sense to involve them in decision making around school improvement. Inspiring them to be engaged in school is an important first step; and teachers have the opportunity to inspire students in a way no one else can!

TEACHER VOICE

I use my teacher voice before my students even arrive for the first day of school by creating a classroom environment that is welcoming, where students are eager to learn and be a part of a community. They can feel the love and know that it is a safe environment in which to learn. On the first day of school, we read books about being peacemakers and make a chart that all students sign to show that they will be peacemakers, too. I know my teacher voice is making a difference when I see my students in action, showing their kindness to each other.

Naomi Discepola, MEd
Kindergarten Teacher
Powers Ferry Elementary School
Cobb County School District
Marietta, Georgia

One can argue that teacher voice is inherently present in the classroom, that it is already influential with students. Agreed—nowhere is teacher voice more readily influential than in the classroom. However, *how* teacher voice is utilized is a critical factor. In general, teacher voice is currently used to direct, order, control, and pace students. This type of voice does little to improve our educational system. On the contrary, it stymies the voices of students and their ability to reach their fullest potential. On the surface, it appears that maintaining "control" in a classroom may be the easier thing to do. Easier? Maybe (although debatable). Better? Not by a long shot. When teacher voice is used solely as an authoritarian tool, classrooms are driven by compliance rather than creativity. We have seen dominance by a teacher weaken the ability of students to accept responsibility for their own learning. The voices of teachers need to change this pattern of behavior from control to collaboration. To do this, the very first step is being willing to listen to students.

MY TEACHER . . .

Chef Tony encourages me to work hard and pursue my dreams. He shows he cares by taking the time to listen to me and understand me as a student. He is a great chef and teaches me valuable lessons that I can use in and outside of school. He taught me the importance of collaboration and teamwork in order by modeling that behavior with us. He also believes in me and gives me experience working in the food industry, side by side with him. While preparing for a big catering event, Chef Tony showed me step by step how to successfully prepare, cook, and serve food. He lets me know what he expects of me, he knows how to support my individual skills, and I won't let him down.

Cali Q (age 14)
Grade 9
Tarpon Springs High School
Pinellas County School District
Tarpon Springs, Florida

Our data tell us that only 52% of students believe teachers are willing to learn from them. This data point becomes even more disheartening when only 47% of students say they have a voice in decision making at school, and this percentage sadly drops from 63% when students are freshmen to 36% when they are seniors. The irony of this is that 97% of teachers claim they encourage students to make decisions, and 83% say they actively seek out the ideas and opinions of students (QISA, 2014; QISA & TVAIC, 2015). The good news is that teachers believe they are doing what is necessary to actively engage students in their learning. The bad news is that students do not believe it is really happening. It is time for teachers to demonstrate to students that they *are* listening, and they appreciate learning from the ideas and opinions of students.

Teachers must seek out students' opinions, creating opportunities to demonstrate to students that they are listening. This is not a passive activity, nor is it simple to implement. But it will inspire students. Schools are typically not structured to support meaningful dialogue on a regular basis. It is challenging, at best, to engage all students in in-depth conversations regularly when you are teaching so many students each day and your time is dictated by a course-driven schedule. The solution? Make listening part of your regular schedule. Protect time to connect with students that is not rushed or superficial. Set up weekly luncheons with students you rarely get to speak with at length. Invite them to your classroom . . . or better yet, eat wherever they typically have lunch. Be ready to pose the following two questions: (1) What can you tell me about how you are learning in your classes? (2) What can we both do differently to make learning more engaging? Then listen.

(And, of course, take notes!) At the first meeting, ask both questions and make a plan with the students for how to implement changes based on their responses to the second questions. At the following week's lunch, discuss how effective the changes were. You may continue this pattern (questions and planning one week, reflection the following week), with these two questions. Or you can invite students to raise their own questions! If shared lunch is out of the question, build 20 minutes into your schedule each week to pose the two questions to your entire class. On the surface, "losing" 20 minutes of instruction may seem like a lot, but it will pay off tenfold. Students will know their teachers are listening to them, and teachers will have a much clearer picture of what is needed to engage students.

It is important during these conversations to not become defensive; be open to learning from what students have to say. Students should know that all feedback is welcome; the best learning will come from the most honest responses. Once you have had time to process the information shared during these conversations, an important next step is to share with students what you heard and how it has impacted your thinking. It is important to be very overt. Sharing what is learned is the very best way to let students know you have listened and are willing to learn from them. This is a critical component in effective collaboration with students.

The next step is determining what to do with what was learned. Listening and learning is great, but it is most effectively utilized when followed by action: listen, learn, and *lead*. Just as students were invited to the table to discuss how things are going and ideas for change, so too should they be involved in the "what next?" discussion. Teachers should not lead in isolation but rather in collaboration with students; both should accept responsibility for the current state of affairs, with a shared obligation to work together to make lasting school improvements.

TEACHER VOICE

It is important to use our teacher voice to advocate for students and to improve our teaching situations. This school year, paraprofessional support was reduced from special classes due to scheduling. Since my principal has made the staff feel safe to talk with her, I voiced my concerns. She addressed my concerns, and advocated for the students by making adjustments, and ensuring IEPs were being implemented. It is vital for student and teacher success that all students and teachers are supported.

Randa Burden
Cobb County School District
Marietta, Georgia

When students are invited to share their ideas as partners in learning, teacher voice moves from lectures to discussions, from leading to facilitating, and from controlling to participating. There is a shift in the classroom environment from being driven by testing and accountability to one of trust and responsibility. This shift inevitably leads to increased engagement in learning—for student and teachers alike. That is the ultimate end game: creating a school culture that honors the voice of all stakeholders and fosters shared responsibility between teachers and students in a manner that helps all achieve their aspirations.

COLLEAGUES

One may consider it natural for teacher voice to be heard and respected among colleagues. Our data say otherwise:

- 71% of teachers believe staff respect each other (compared to 91% of staff believing that students respect them).
- 68% of teachers feel comfortable asking questions in staff meetings.
- 65% of teachers say they are excited to tell their colleagues when they do something well. (QISA, 2014; QISA & TVAIC, 2015)

This is a problem! For teacher voice to be effective, teachers must be willing to listen and learn from one another. This is nearly impossible if there is an underlying lack of respect and a fear of raising questions. Add to that the fact that teachers are reluctant to share their efforts and successes.

Some light is shed on the data above when you realize that only 48% of the teachers claim they communicate effectively in their schools (QISA & TVAIC, 2015). Sobering data indeed. We have written for years about the importance of communication and positive relationships between students and teachers. It is impossible for students to ever have a voice if they cannot communicate with and be heard by teachers. And so it is between colleagues—they must be able to communicate effectively with each other in order to work effectively together. A change in culture is needed, and it is needed now.

For a group of individuals who communicate for a living, teachers do not communicate very well with one another. They need to develop better habits of communicating with colleagues. Jim Knight's (2016) better conversation habits, referenced in Chapter 4, should certainly be applied when communicating with colleagues. Knight believes that effective communication is as much about the beliefs you work from as it is about the way you act. To us, this means that the voice of teachers needs to be genuine. Say what you mean and mean what you say . . . then act accordingly. Teachers may *say* they value the importance of their voice; however, if they do not demonstrate respect for the voice of their colleagues, their communication with others will become shallow and meaningless. Knight

I have never experienced my teacher voice not being heard. However, I have witnessed how it affects other teachers, and how they do not feel valued when their voice goes unheard. To do my part, I make sure peers' voices are heard by sharing their ideas within professional development and learning communities. While sharing ideas at lunchtime or walking in the hallway, I always give credit where credit is due, and then I inform that teacher that his or her ideas were shared. It's always a great feeling to hear your colleague say, "Wow, you thought that was a good enough idea to share with others?"

Rekia Beverly
Chisholm Elementary
Volusia County Schools
New Smyrna Beach, Florida

believes that effective communication involves figuring out first what we believe, then working to make sure that what we do reflects those beliefs. A key take away for teachers from Knight's book is that one cannot presume that effective conversations come naturally. It takes purposeful effort to be a good communicator and put into action a set of habits that reflect your own beliefs.

Improved communication, based on educators' true beliefs, can simultaneously improve respect and enhance the support network among colleagues. If educators believe in the value of high-achieving teachers who make a meaningful difference for students, then their words and related actions should show unwavering support when teachers are acknowledged for just that. One of the saddest things to witness in education is seeing what happens to the Teacher of the Year. While such accomplishment should be celebrated, cherished, and learned from, it often results in alienation and resentment for the recipient. Some even perceive the teacher as being "in it" for all the wrong reasons. That is petty thinking, but all too often a reality in today's school culture. Why are teachers seemingly threatened by other teachers' successes? Rather than a threat, there should be an embrace.

Embracing a colleague's success and learning from it is much more productive for everyone. Teaching should be a collaborative endeavor. It should be commonplace for teachers to share ideas and provide feedback. The "open door policy" should not apply just to administrators, but to colleagues as well. And teachers should abide by one of the skills students learn in preschool: share. Share ideas, successes, and struggles. Teachers should share what is happening in classrooms throughout the school and be willing to accept feedback and offer helpful insights to their colleagues. There is perhaps no greater compliment and motivational tool than the praise received from an individual who understands, values, and is committed to the same profession.

While teachers have the ability to motivate other teachers, it is imperative to keep in mind that there are two underlying aspects that must be present to establish a foundation for effective communication and ultimately motivation: trust and respect. With this, teachers will feel comfortable voicing their honest opinions with their colleagues. Teachers will feel respected for their unique ideas and talent, while knowing that they share common goals for the school with their colleagues. This is the way forward in order for teacher voice to flourish.

LEADERSHIP

For too long, the idea of strengthening teacher voice had sent shudders down a principal's spine. No surprise. Teacher voice has long been associated with complaining, grievances, and the union. No more. Teacher voice needs to be filled with ideas, hope, and pride. Teacher voice will be held in higher regard, and more genuinely listened to, by principals and other school and district leaders when it is infused with suggestions for improvement rather than griping about the status quo. Comments such as "We do not do that here," or "We tried that before and it was a

TEACHER VOICE

It can be difficult to find your voice when talking to administration, especially if they are set in their ways. When you try to talk with them, sometimes all you hear from them is that "It has always been done this way" or "At my old school, we did it this way," which can make it difficult to affect change. My students needed more course options to choose from, but we kept being told that there were not enough teachers to implement a change in course offerings. I decided to fight for what we needed. Once I had all my facts organized, I went to the administrator and discussed the reasons we need more options, the solutions to his concerns, and how it could be a positive change for the school. I listened and addressed all questions but held firm to making it clear that this was a much needed change. We now offer several more classes due to my voice being positive, proactive, and heard.

Nikki Bisesi
Science Teacher
Department Chair & AP Coordinator
Hillgrove High School
Cobb County School District
Powder Springs, Georgia

waste of time," need to be replaced with "Let's give it a try," and "What can I do to make sure we do not make the same mistakes again?" The latter approach represents an attitude of hope and an aptitude for change—a willingness to identify areas in need of improvement and suggest concrete ways to make the improvements. Such an approach, in contrast to whining, demonstrates a sense of commitment to success within the school and pride in all that can be accomplished.

For teacher voice to work collaboratively with leadership, the communication must be consistent. Regularly scheduled staff meetings are a typical venue for exercising voice, but they are certainly not the only way, and we would argue not even the best way. Teachers need to be proactive. Invite leadership to visit your classroom. Meet with those in positions of authority before or after school over coffee (or tea, or seltzer . . .). The key is to have meaningful *conversations*. Such dialogue occurs when we follow some additional rules we learned at an early age in school and on the playground: Take turns and respect others. Both parties should share ideas *and listen* to each other. A conversation monopolized by one person is not a conversation at all—that's a lecture. What is needed is consistent, meaningful dialogue in an atmosphere of goodwill. This serves to establish mutual trust and respect, the foundation on which collaboration can thrive.

Such communication should be approached with a supportive mindset, a desire to build up rather than tear down, and the belief that we are all in this together. Teacher voice will never be fully realized with leadership if there is a "we versus them" mentality. The sooner teachers and those in positions of authority embrace genuine collaboration, the sooner administrators will encourage teacher voice and utilize it for school improvement.

It is important to keep in mind that sharing teacher voice with school and district leaders does not automatically mean all thoughts and ideas will be accepted. That would be called "getting your way" instead of "sharing your voice." Talking to those in leadership positions is an opportunity to open a channel of communication, one that is largely overlooked. Establishing regular communication with the principal and other leaders builds greater trust and respect between teachers and the administration. Remember, you are all in this together, with a shared goal.

This may all seem too "kumbaya-ish", but it's true. And in case it seems too easily achieved, it is important to note that there is an initial mountain to climb here. Currently, only 67% of teachers believe the building administration is open to new ideas. Even more disturbing is that the fact that only 60% of teachers think principals are willing to learn from them (QISA & TVAIC, 2015). As asserted in Chapter 3, fully integrating teacher voice in schools requires teacher and organizational readiness. It is not the sole responsibility of administration. However, if one is to expect teachers to have a voice, principals and other administrators must be genuinely willing and able to listen to and learn from the teaching staff. And their readiness must be crystal clear to the teachers!

As for teachers' responsibility, they need to take their voice out of the shadows and engage in respectful dialogue. No more out-of-earshot conversations about what is not working at school and the administration's role in that. It is imperative that teachers stop using their voice to talk about someone, and start talking *with* someone. Teachers must be open about their concerns *and* their ideas for making things better. The former without the latter can be perceived as complaining; the two together demonstrate a vested interest in improving the teaching and learning environment.

PARENTS

Teachers certainly have a voice with parents, but it typically comes in one of two modes: defense or offense. Neither achieves the kind of voice we are advocating for. Teachers often find themselves being criticized or questioned by parents and use their voice in response in a defensive manner. On the flip side of the coin, teachers go on the offense with parents when calling to notify them of a disciplinary issue or academic concern. Similar to communicating with administrators, conversations with parents should occur on a regular basis, in an open and respectful manner, and include productive solution-oriented dialogue.

One of the best ways to enhance communication between parents and teachers is to broaden the conversation. It should go beyond grades, attendance, and discipline issues. Discussions should be about more than what is *not* going well! There should be regular conversations that celebrate progress and generate an exchange of ideas regarding how to best support students. Teachers need to use their voice to tell parents about their child's successes in school and share what they know about the child's hopes and dreams for the future. In turn, parents will share what they believe their child's hopes and dreams are. Such dialogue shifts the conversations from an authoritarian feel to one of collaboration, working together to determine how to best motivate students and help them achieve their aspirations. One question that is a failsafe approach with parents is: "How can we work together for the betterment of your child?" Ask this, and we promise you will be impressed with what you learn.

In addition to broadening the topic of conversations with parents, teachers must be conscious about adjusting conversations to align with the needs of the particular parents they are speaking with. Teachers can tend to use the same tone and educational jargon for all audiences. They need to be cognizant that while some parents love speaking with teachers, others are greatly unnerved by it, even fearing it. Some parents will be up to date on the most recent initiatives in education, while others depend on the teacher to provide any relevant information to them. For teacher voice to be effective with parents, teachers must be aware of their varying audience and adjust their conversations accordingly. (For example, it may be helpful to avoid acronyms. Telling a parent about an ASCD conference attended for PD to ensure her child is making AYP, and that it is important to meet the ESSA (formerly NCLB)

TEACHER VOICE

I send home positivity postcards for two students each week. The postcards compliment the students on their positive contributions to the classroom and their dedication to their own learning, including specific examples. The postcards let the parents and students know that I notice them, encourage them, and I am thankful for them. The postcards are not just for high achieving students. I especially like to recognize students who are struggling and have had a personal achievement or made a special effort. Parents love to receive positive feedback. It encourages open communication and parent/teacher team bonding.

Patsy Kraj
ESOL Science Teacher
Wheeler High School
Cobb County School District
Marietta, Georgia

requirements, which will be discussed with the IEP at the upcoming PET meeting, may not be informative, or even helpful!) Parents want to hear from teachers in a language they understand. Being an engaged listener during conversations with parents, and listening to their responses to your own questions, will allow you to gauge and adjust your own tone, wording, and message effectively.

There are certainly circumstances that teachers can and probably should be defensive about, and there are certainly times teachers need to go on the offense. But generally speaking, communication with parents (the way teacher voice is intended) needs to be much more consistent, frequent, and positive in order to avoid being perceived as aggressive or defensive and instead be embraced as collaborative.

We know that 93% of students say their parents care about their education (QISA, 2014). We also believe that all parents want what is best for their own child. Granted, parents may not be "caring" for their children in a manner that matches what a teacher believes is best for their academic development, but nonetheless, parents *do* care and want a great future for their child. Teachers should never lose sight of that fact. For teacher voice to be effective, it is critical to take time to understand and honor the parents of the students you are teaching. This not only strengthens direct communication with parents but also allows teachers to develop a better understanding of the students in their classroom. Parent-teacher communication is key to developing a partnership that ultimately enhances the students' learning experience.

For this to truly take hold, teachers must initiate conversations. You cannot wait for parents to approach you. The most challenging scenario is communicating

I sit in IEP meetings with parents who often seem uncomfortable with the setting and jargon. I bring a pen and paper so they can take notes. I also bring tissues and strategically sit next to them. I stop the psychological evaluator as he rattles off test names, percentages, and standard deviations and ask him to clarify and explain. When he finishes, I turn to the family and say "His test did not measure how kind Sam is or how successful we know he will be. You have heard he has challenges, and now you will hear how we want to create solutions with you."

Ashley Bryant Reynolds, MSEd
2nd Grade Teacher
Captain Albert Stevens School
Regional School Unit #71
Belfast, Maine

with parents who do not particularly like school (often because of negative experiences as students themselves). Assuming all parents want to enter the school and talk with teachers is naive. Teachers must be mobile, willing to go to the parents and meet in a location they are comfortable with—a coffee shop, a park bench—anywhere that is not in or near the building they have a strong aversion to. Teachers need to make an effort to reach out to parents who do not naturally reach out to them.

Once communication starts, teachers will be better served to listen more than they speak. Find out what the parents' concerns are for their children, both in and outside of the school. Let parents know you genuinely care about their child and want what is best for that child. When the meeting does involve an issue that needs to be addressed, make sure a plan is in place before the meeting wraps up—a straightforward plan where you and the parent work together for the same cause, supporting the child.

One caution when it comes to working with parent groups: Teachers must be aware that no matter how well-intentioned a group may be, they may not represent the entire student body. In one district we worked with, the parent group was incredibly supportive of the school and genuinely wanted to be involved. At the first meeting, we were extremely impressed with their ideas about what was needed and how they could support school efforts. The next day, we went into the schools and realized that the parent group represented only a small portion of student body, and their efforts were focused on supporting their own children.

We certainly advocate for teachers sharing their voice with parent groups and for parental involvement in schools. However, in situations where the group does not represent the entire student body, teacher voice must be utilized to broaden the advisory board's understanding of what is occurring within the school for all students. Teachers are responsible for providing the best education possible for *every* child, not just the ones whose parents are strong advocates.

COMMUNITY

Too often we define "involving the community" as including the parents. Yes, parents are an invaluable component, but caring and involvement are not restricted to those whose children attend the schools. There are many additional community members who are committed to the success of local schools. Teacher voice can have an influence on community members who are eager to collaborate and contribute—residents, local businesses, elected representatives, charitable organizations, and clubs, to name a few. All are invested in the success of the community and in the success of the students. From retired grandparents to business executives, all community members deserve to be listened to, and they are an invaluable resource for teachers—both to learn from and collaborate with.

It is critical to strengthen relationships between teachers and community members by "flipping" the current model of community partnerships. Too often, community involvement has been about schools asking for assistance, such as donations, from organizations. Turn this approach on its head! Teachers should ask community members what schools can do *for them*. Talents and skills abound in our schools. Teachers can share their talents (and those of their students) with others in the community. This helps the community see schools as an integral part of the community rather than organizations designed to educate students in isolation. It also demonstrates that teachers (and indeed everyone who works in schools!) are not only critical to the lives of the students they teach, but are a valuable and resourceful part of the larger community.

Sharing teacher voice within the community also counterbalances the abundance of information shared in today's media-rich society. Too frequently, the stories that go viral are the ones that cast a less favorable light on schools: contract issues, strikes, teacher pay, and sometimes illegal behavior. Sadly, the upbeat stories about educators do not get the same traction. It's time to turn this around as well! Share with your community all the positive efforts that are made in your school—by you and your students! Provide examples of innovation, motivation, and collaboration. Be purposeful and positive about your message to the public; schools are full of positive and inspiring stories. Find ways to make these the stories go viral!

As strong connections are made, relationships are built, and experiences are shared, true partnerships can form. The benefits are multifaceted. The community is able to see the positive aspects of school, and partnerships develop in a manner that is beneficial for all involved. Schools *are* an integral part of the community and should be acknowledged as such—a part of the community that can both contribute to and benefit from collaborative efforts with other community members. It is a win-win situation: renewed respect for the teaching and learning community within schools and a more engaged, cohesive, and supportive community overall. Community members and schools are alive with ideas, insights, and resources that are mutually beneficial. The question to ask, really, is what can we do *together*? Use your voice to drive positive change!

As you proceed, keep this in mind: Just as it is important to understand your parents in order to communicate effectively, so it is with community members. Each community member has a different perspective and level of experience with schools. Some may have backgrounds in education and know every acronym under the sun! Others have not seen the inside of a school in decades. Be patient and embrace these differences. There is an immense amount that can be learned from various perspectives. Conversations with community members are a perfect opportunity for teachers to listen a great deal more than they speak.

While listening to the various ideas throughout the community, it is important to simultaneously be aware of the larger context. For example, a retiree's primary concern may be the bottom line of the budget given that they are on a fixed income and are nervous about rising taxes; an unemployed individual may think teachers are overpaid (not to mention they get summers off!); the business person may claim teachers are not graduating sufficiently prepared students whom he/she can hire; the local minister may suggest that young people in school today have no sense of social obligation. Teachers may come up against some difficult scenarios within community forums, but there is always something that can be learned. The best piece of advice is to be prepared for such a situation and to not automatically take a defensive stance or abruptly go on the offense. Rather, teachers should genuinely listen and seek to understand each perspective. At the same time, teachers should be ready to share their own voice with confidence and provide examples that demonstrate what is really occurring in schools. Teachers need to make a commitment to understanding various perspectives and experiences so they are better equipped to meet community members where they are and join forces to move forward in collaborative efforts to improve schools, and indeed the entire community.

School board meetings are a natural forum for community outreach, a staple within school systems that provides a consistent platform for sharing your voice. Given their stable presence and the fact that school boards are comprised of well-intentioned community members (admittedly, sometimes with a few exceptions!), this is a valuable forum for teachers to share their voice *on a consistent basis*. In general, this may understandably not be the most exhilarating event of choice after a full day of teaching. However, teachers' regular attendance is an opportunity to guide the discussion in a positive and productive direction. Teachers should request five minutes at each meeting, preferably toward the beginning, to provide an update of new and exciting initiatives at their school. This is an opportunity to be proactive, to express teachers' views and concerns (coupled with ideas for solutions!) before they become larger issues. The very best way to avoid the snowball effect with problems is to have consistent communication about what is happening!

At every board meeting, teachers should have the opportunity to share what they are most proud of, what has occurred since the last meeting, and voice current concerns. Yes, teachers should go ahead and share it all (respectfully, of course) . . . the good, the bad, and the ugly. It is important to paint a true picture of schools in order to make meaningful progress. Teachers need to be transparent and genuine if there is going to be productive dialogue with board members. As long as communication is approached in a respectful manner and trust is fostered alongside the mutual goal of improving teaching and learning for everyone, then progress will follow. And once teachers are comfortable, they can go one step further and ask students to join them. Together, they can demonstrate the pride they have in what is being accomplished at school!

We believe the most challenging audience for sharing teacher voice is the public, outside of the daily school environment. However, nothing is more rewarding or beneficial when it is done well. Consider it the biggest catch of the season!

The potential for teacher voice is unlimited. To tap into this potential, teachers must create opportunities to foster their voice. Go ahead and cast a line. Just like

TEACHER VOICE

Teacher voice thrives on opportunity and action! Serving as a Foundation board member, I have worked with community representatives for the past four years. When our work began, I was startled to find out how little they knew of the 21st century classroom, teacher, or student. My role has evolved within our board to be *the voice* for the needs of our school beyond the traditional thinking that these board members experienced as students. Being actively involved has been crucial in the success of various programs, including a student-centered collaborative learning classroom.

Jodi Bitler
6th Grade Social Studies Teacher
Durham Middle School
Cobb County School District
Acworth, Georgia

	STUDENTS	COLLEAGUES	LEADERS	PARENTS	COMMUNITY
Listen	"I am protecting time for discussions with my students on things that matter *to them*."	"I am visiting and observing my fellow teachers in action."	"I am entering meetings with leadership in an open-minded manner."	"I am calling parents on a regular basis to share good news about their children."	"I am attending local organizations such as Rotary and the Elks Club."
Learn	"My past is not their present."	"Some of the very best teachers are in my own building, and I can learn a lot from them."	"We are on the same team. We just need to learn to 'play' better together."	"All parents want what is best for their child."	"The community may not truly understand the challenges schools face on a day-to-day basis. I can change that."
Lead	"I am ensuring my classes are relevant to my students' hopes and dreams."	"I am incorporating new teaching techniques in my classroom that I have learned from colleagues."	"I am collaborating with the principal and providing more ideas than concerns!"	"My role has changed from telling parents what to do, to working as partners as we guide students in the right direction."	"I am taking an active role when it comes to public relations, sharing all the good things we are doing in school!"

fishing, it takes patience, persistence, and a little determination to achieve success. And while the outcome is sometimes unpredictable, it is always worth the effort, because there is something that can be learned each time.

Action Steps to Foster the Influence of Teacher Voice

- **Model teacher voice.** Teachers are inherently role models and are constantly being emulated by students. The challenge is to be the best role model you can be and use your voice to encourage students to utilize theirs. Using kind words that promote openness and acceptance will more effectively cultivate conversations with students than a tone that denotes authority and control. Modeling has a greater impact than preaching.

- **Stop the sarcasm.** Teachers may think they are being funny with their quick quips, using sarcasm as a way to get a laugh from students. However, there is a fine line between being funny and being disrespectful. Sarcasm, in most instances, crosses that line and often invites sarcasm from students. Be real, be funny, be yourself, but omit the sarcasm.

- **Build bridges by visiting classrooms.** Teachers expect classroom visits from evaluators for formal observations, but rarely do colleagues visit each other's classes while they are in progress. Understandably, it may be initially difficult to teach in front of your colleagues, but the opportunity to reflect and share best practices in an informal manner is invaluable. Teachers need to get out of the assessment mindset and become comfortable sharing ideas and learning from each other in a safe and nurturing environment.

- **Socialize new teachers.** One can never assume that new teachers know how to communicate with their colleagues. Most teacher education programs educate teachers about how to communicate with students but fall short of teaching them how to communicate with other teachers. Never assume teachers inherently know how to communicate with their colleagues within the school setting. Spend time at the beginning of the school year discussing various modes of effective collegial communication, as well as the expectations the school has for teachers using their voice.

- **Ask questions.** The best way to learn from the administration is to ask questions. Keep in mind that the phrasing of questions matters. It is a bit of an art form. Enter the conversation with an open mind and respectful tone. Instead of asking, "Where did you come up with an idea like that?" ask, "Can you help me understand your rationale for this decision?" Asking questions that put the administration on the defensive will only prompt defensive responses.

- **Be the initiator.** Let the principal know you want to talk to him/her. Go in with a plan of *communication*, not a plan of attack. Share your thoughts and be prepared to offer solutions for your concerns, demonstrating that you are ready to take action to make things better. There may be times when you do not have concerns, but it is still important to continue to meet with the principal regularly. This fosters open communication for all occasions—celebrating successes and brainstorming solutions for identified issues—and provides routine opportunities to discuss either.

- **Avoid assumptions.** Do not enter a conversation with the principal thinking she is the voice of all things evil. Principals are people, too; they are just as vulnerable and sensitive as teachers. They may not show it publically, but rest assured, they can possess the same insecurities as the rest of us. Similarly, do not assume the principal does not want to listen to you. Enter the conversation with optimism, confidence, and a productive plan.

- **Broaden conversations with parents.** Instead of talking to parents only about their child's grades, discipline issues, or attendance, ask parents about the personal side of their child. Listen to what parents have to say about what motivates their child. In turn, share with parents what has been learned at school about their child's aspirations. Teachers may be surprised to find out that some parents are not aware of all that their child is interested in or dreams of achieving. Teachers have an amazing opportunity to impact the relationship between parents and students by using their voice.

- **Attend community forums and offer to help.** If teachers want their voices to be heard in the community, they need to capitalize on opportunities. There are endless possibilities, but teachers must show up at the venues where there is a platform for their voice. In addition to school board meetings, we suggest attending meetings at the Rotary, Elks Club, VFW, and various places of worship. Reach out to local businesses to meet with their leaders, offering to collaborate on projects that impact the community. Let the community know how committed teachers are to the development and learning of young people and growth of the community overall. Too often the default button for teachers is to ask for something from community members. We suggest you hit the reset button. Offer your ideas and insights for working *together*. Articulate the skills and ideas that you and your students bring to the table. You will find, as trusted relationships develop, that your voice is not only welcome, but ultimately sought out. The potential for productive collaboration between schools and community members is powerful. Let your voice be a driving force!

Teacher Reflections

1. Do you understand your audience within the community, including parents, and communicate effectively with them?

2. How are you consistently using your voice within the community?

3. How is your voice a role model for students?

4. In what ways does your voice highlight the positive aspects of your school? How does your voice create opportunities for further improvement?

5. With which groups are you most comfortable sharing your voice? Why? How can you challenge yourself to use your voice outside of your comfort zone?

CHAPTER 6

Teacher Voice and Technology

Technology gives teacher voice a platform to be heard by the world.

The notion of either of us writing a chapter on technology is somewhat ironic, because neither of us would be self-described tech-savvy individuals. Don't get us wrong, we do have some skills in this area: We both type, use Skype, and are active on Twitter. One of us even uses an electronic calendar, and the other loves to shop online. (Do not let gender bias fool you in determining who does which on this one!) Most importantly, we are both perpetual learners and are continually picking up new tech skills from our colleagues, teachers we work with, and most frequently from our kids!

Then again, maybe our middle-of-the-road tech savviness will allow us to explore the connection between teacher voice and technology from an interesting viewpoint. We recognize the incredible and increasingly pervasive role technology plays in life, and we support effective use of digital tools as resources to enhance the learning experience. We *do not* believe that technology is the answer to everything, and most importantly, we do not believe for a second that technology will replace teachers. We do think it is possible that in the future, teachers who effectively use technology will replace those who do not. And we most certainly believe that technology can be a powerful tool for amplifying teacher voice.

Fullan and Quinn write in their book *Coherence: The Right Drivers in Action for Schools, Districts, and Systems,* "Traditional schooling is increasingly generating bored and alienated students and teachers. The allure of digital and better engaging pedagogy is combining to disrupt existing classrooms" (2016, p. 73). When used appropriately, technology can play a powerful role in transforming learning. It can facilitate connectivity in ways unimaginable only a few years ago. Fullan and Quinn go on to cite Schmidt and Cohen (2013) stating, "The form of connectivity doubles roughly every nine months . . . the promise of exponential growth unleashes possibilities in graphics and virtual reality that will make the online experience as real as real life, or perhaps even better" (p. 82). Technology is a remarkable and enduring part of our present and future. Using technology is no longer a superfluous skill to develop when leisure time allows. It has become an integral part of navigating through today's world and an essential skill in order to maximize potential within this ever-changing landscape. Teachers have an incredible opportunity to employ technology to amplify their voice, a chance to tell their story and expand their influence as educators.

■ ■ ■ TECHNOLOGY & TEACHER VOICE

Educators are always looking for a silver bullet when it comes to teaching and learning. The fact is, there isn't just one . . . there are many. Technology in education is a game changer. It has, and will continue to have, a profound impact on the teaching and learning experience. Technology has the power to unlock the potential in all students and teachers to express their voice and impact a significant audience. When leveraged properly, technology is used to consume and create, opening limitless doors for learning and leading. Technology has the ability to fundamentally change how we see and hear teacher and student voice.

Dan Massimino
10 Years in Education (Former 5th Grade Teacher)
Associate Director
Center for School Improvement & Policy Studies
Boise State University
Boise, Idaho ■

The relationship between teacher voice and technology can be considered through the School Voice Model: Listen, Learn, and Lead. Educators have unprecedented access to people, ideas, and resources through the vast array of online platforms. The possibilities are truly endless for teachers to listen, learn, and lead with their voice in virtual spaces, ultimately amplifying their voice both in and outside of those virtual spaces.

LISTEN

A colossal amount of information is at our fingertips at any given moment. One no longer needs to wait for the library to open, or the newspaper to be delivered, or for the evening news to air in order to find out what is happening in the world. The answer to most any question can be found within seconds on a device small enough to fit in the palm of your hand . . . or even on your wrist! Clearly there are incredible benefits of having such limitless access to information. However, new challenges now exist as individuals attempt to sort through the abundance of resources, determine what is accurate, and focus on resources with personal and professional value. In his book *Too Big to Know: Rethinking Knowledge Now That the Facts Aren't the Facts, Experts Are Everywhere, and the Smartest Person in the Room Is the Room*, Dave Weinberger declares that we are in a crisis of knowledge. "Everyone with any stupid idea has a megaphone as big as that of educated, trained people. We form 'echo chambers' online and actually encounter fewer challenges to our thinking than we did during the broadcast era" (2011, p. xii). There is *plenty* of information out there, and a multitude of voices. Teachers must exercise critical thinking in determining what they should spend their time listening to. This is also an opportunity to model for students the process of locating and listening to sources that are valid and will most support them in achieving their aspirations.

Weinberger is not all doom and gloom about the impact of the Internet; in fact, the premise of his work is that the smartest person in the room is now the room itself when the people within it connect their ideas, both within that room and beyond. "Our task is to learn how to build smart rooms—that is, how to build networks that make us smarter, especially since, when done badly, networks can make us distressingly stupider" (2011, p. xiii). Developing a solid professional learning network that taps into people and resources available via technology can literally be life changing in the professional life of a teacher. They key is to be tuned in and listening to the right channels.

75% of teachers say they receive constructive
feedback from colleagues.

BUILDING YOUR NETWORK

A Professional Learning Network (PLN) is a community of people, organizations, and resources utilized to advance one's learning. PLN's used to be limited to those who could be contacted in person, by phone, and eventually by e-mail. Now, the sky is the limit! Using platforms such as Twitter, blogs, webcasts, and so on, one can communicate with and tap into the insights of experts who had previously been logistically challenging to connect with. There are no longer boundaries associated with geography or time. As Will Richardson and Rob Mancabelli state in their book *Professional Learning Networks: Using the Power of Connections to Transform Education,* "We can learn on a particular topic at a particular time or simply tap into an ongoing stream of knowledge from which we can sip anytime we like" (2011, p. 2). Teachers can exercise their voice literally anytime and from anywhere in the world with Internet access.

TEACHER VOICE THROUGH TWITTER

Twitter has been embraced by many teachers and has had a profound impact on their ability to express their voice. A teacher's PLN, especially through Twitter, is available 24/7. Perusing Twitter for lesson ideas on a Monday morning, engaging in classroom management discussions on a Friday night with teachers from around the world, or exploring the latest education articles from leading scholars on a Sunday morning in your pajamas are all possible with Twitter. Twitter allows teachers to ask their PLN for assistance, to share practices, and seek new ideas at any place and at any time.

Eric Nichols
17 Years in Education (Former High School Social Studies Teacher)
Director of School Improvement
Harney Education Service District
Burns, Oregon

A few thoughts to consider when building a PLN or reflecting on the effectiveness of an existing network to amplify teacher voice:

1. **Let Aspirations Drive the Network.** When considering *who* and *what* to listen to within the PLN, consider the following question as an initial filter: Will the information I am listening to help me reach my personal and professional aspirations? If the answer is no, then "cut bait"! This does *not* mean one should only listen to perspectives that match their own. Far from it! Listening to opposing points of view is an informative and healthy approach to learning. The determining factor should be whether or not what is being listened to *has a productive impact* on the journey to achieving professional aspirations.

2. **Be Selective.** There is no magic size for your professional learning network, but it is advisable to be selective and limit it to what can be effectively managed. Fullan and Quinn point out that, "One downside for users is finding a way to keep track of the deluge of information and to avoid the distraction of interesting but not necessarily relevant information" (2016, p. 70–71). For example, a Twitter feed with a million connections may cause you to miss information coming from a select few that could have the greatest impact on your thinking. Consider using tools such as HootSuite or TweetDeck to follow individual hashtags and conversations.

And do not be afraid to modify the PLN over time. As a teacher's interests and knowledge base evolve, so should his or her network. Those that are no longer significantly contributing to the journey should be pulled from your tackle box, and new entities that will enhance professional growth and insight should be added.

3. **Make Connections.** While judiciously determining *what* to listen to, it is important to simultaneously consider *how* to connect the information that is heard. Consideration must be given to how the insights and knowledge gained can impact teacher voice, classroom practices, and professional aspirations. Intentionally including diverse thinking in a PLN, including from different fields of study, will serve to fortify the overall experience. Key takeaways from PLN participation should serve to foster teachers' aspirations and inspire them to take action.

4. **Consume and Contribute.** Listening is a key first step, but one must be continually cognizant of what is being learned, the professional impact it has, and how to contribute back to the PLN. Stopping after the listening stage is a missed opportunity to exercise teacher voice. The power of a PLN is optimized when one engages in conversation, shares resources, and contributes to the collective learning of the network. When teachers become better networked, they gain visibility and influence. Other people will start listening! But now we are getting ahead of ourselves. More to come on learning and leading in shortly . . .

■ ■ ■ CONSIDERATIONS FOR BUILDING OR REFLECTING ON YOUR PLN

1. Let Aspirations Drive the Network
2. Be Selective
3. Make Connections
4. Consume and Contribute ■

Establishing a strong PLN will allow teachers to meaningfully engage with individuals and resources invested in education anytime, anywhere. When teachers are listening to the right channels, PNL's provide a platform from which teachers can strengthen their voice and sense of purpose.

One of the resources we used to stay connected with other educators for ongoing, meaningful conversations around transforming teaching and learning is the Corwin Connected Educators group. Join the conversation at #CorwinCE and explore examples of how connectedness can enhance learning at http://www.corwin.com/connectededucators/.

Tom Whitby, who spent 34 years as a high school English teacher, has a site dedicated to supporting personal learning networks for educators. You can connect with over 17,000 educators in this network at http://edupln.ning.com/. ■

LEARN

Clearly, listening and learning are connected. Whether the interaction is facilitated by technology or not, whether the expression is spoken, tweeted, or typed, educators have the opportunity to learn something new every time they listen to another individual. Technology, in addition to providing progressive opportunities to connect with others and enhance dialogue, provides unprecedented access to educational tools and resources.

The days of having to drive to the local teacher supply store and spend hours perusing the aisles in search of the most recent resources, agonizing over which teaching tools would be most worthy of the limited funds available (frequently out of a teacher's own pocket) are long gone. In the context of a focus group, one teacher shared with us, "I never buy education resources in a store anymore. I can literally find any education resource I want online, and most of it is free!" Teachers are no longer limited to their old tackle box of curriculum materials and file cabinets jammed with laminated lesson plans! We know that there are still great offerings to be found in teacher supply stores and in packaged curriculum materials. And yes, filing cabinets (physical and virtual) still exist for organizing relevant materials. Our point is that resources are now more readily available and are constantly current!

The ability to learn from other people and resources used to be limited by geography and time. The growth of open resource materials for teachers and students alike, as well as networks within Learning Management Systems (LMS) such as Edmodo and Schoology that keep everyone connected, have changed all that. Teachers now have immediately accessible platforms to collaborate with a global audience and the ability to personalize conversations and resources to match their specific interests and needs. This shift has had a dramatic impact on the ability of teachers to continually learn, add to their content knowledge base, refine pedagogical practices, and express their voice in meaningful ways.

INFORMATION ACCESS

ACCESS IN THE PAST	ACCESS IN THE PRESENT
Limited by Geography and Time	Anywhere, Anytime
Local Collaboration	Global Collaboration
Generalized Resources	Personalized Resources
Waiting for Information	Information in Real Time
Information Flows One Way	Information Flows Both Ways
Received Information From Experts	*You* Become the Expert

Opportunities to learn are literally endless. Teachers can still pull the handle on the filing cabinet drawer, but they can also click on folders to engage in electronic sharing of resources through platforms such as Google Docs, DropBox, and Pinterest. Resources can still be purchased in stores, provided in curriculum kits, and checked out from local libraries; but they can also be accessed anytime online with filter options to personalize a search by categories such as grade level, content area, and lesson topic.

The online world has also had significant impact on professional development possibilities. In-person professional development continues to play a critical role in ongoing learning of teachers, but additional opportunities now exist online, from degree programs to Massive Online Open Courses (MOOC) as well as lectures and lessons on particular topics from platforms such as Kahn Academy and TED Talks.

One example of an institution of higher education that is blazing the way in embracing online learning is Southern New Hampshire University (SNHU). SNHU is rethinking education and capitalizing on technology, now offering over 180 different online programs to more than 34,000 students. Slate has referred to SNHU as the "Amazon of higher education" because they continue to grow their online presence, while maintaining a "customer service" approach to supporting their students (Kahn, 2014). Thanks to advances in technology, the limits to learning continue to diminish.

Teachers, and students, truly have unprecedented access to tools and resources that can strengthen their learning. With that comes a responsibility—skillfully searching through tremendous amounts of information to determine relevance of the material and validity of the source. This is an important step in this technologically enhanced world in which we live. With so much to choose from, it is important to make conscious decisions about who to listen to and ultimately learn from.

As teachers work to amplify their voice, it is critical to listen and learn; and then step up to lead!

LEAD

Technology provides endless opportunities to listen and learn . . . (And sometimes get distracted! We have admittedly spent significant time viewing YouTube videos of giant fish being reeled in and researching our own dream destinations for the next big catch!) Distractions aside, to truly harness the potential impact of technology on teacher voice, teachers must go one step further; they must use technology to *lead*. Technology can and should serve as an amplifier for teacher voice.

■■■ AMPLIFYING TEACHER VOICE THROUGH TECHNOLOGY

In our district, teachers who utilize technology to amplify their voices use social media to make their work public, as well as to connect and engage in meaningful dialogue with colleagues across the state, country, and world. These educators embrace the opportunity to showcase the great work they are doing every day with their students; they use platforms such as class blogs, Twitter, and even e-mail to engage with a global audience beyond the classroom walls. They also participate in Twitter chats such as #edchat and #mnlead, exploring, sharing, and learning with a network of fellow lifelong learners and leaders.

Andrew Hamilton
9 Years in Education (Former High School English Teacher)
Technology Integration Specialist
Northeast Metro Intermediate School District
White Bear Lake, Minnesota ■

Using teacher voice to lead in virtual spaces is about more than establishing a presence on social media or learning how to use the latest and greatest platforms and apps. It is about knowing who you are as an educator, carefully crafting what you want to express, and purposefully using your voice to share that message. In writing about how to strategically use technology to transform school culture, Eric Sheninger defines digital leadership as the "consistent pursuit of innovation, effective integration of technology, quality professional development, transparency, celebration of successes from which others may learn, establishment of relationships with stakeholders, an open mind, and anticipation of continued change" (2014, p. 23). It requires a mindset that technology can enhance efforts to continually improve the teaching and learning experience for students and teachers.

With this mindset, teachers can lead with their voice by sharing their current practices, unique ideas, and resources and encouraging others to work collaboratively to do the same. Sheninger goes on to say, "As good ideas travel swiftly through social media channels, they will be embraced and implemented by others looking to initiate sustainable change" (2014, p.185). The use of technology will expand the reach and influence of teacher voice. Others will listen to and learn from teachers as they share their ideas and embrace opportunities to lead, both within their school and the virtual world.

> *79% of teachers see themselves as a leader, but only*
> *61% believe their colleagues see them as a leader.*

TEACHER BRAND AND DIGITAL FOOTPRINTS

Along with the rise of technology has come the increased focus on branding, the concept of putting out there who you are as an individual or organization. "At its core, a brand is a purposeful engagement in a public conversation, a strategic effort to showcase what you're proud of—what makes you special as an educator. Teachers have an enormous opportunity to take charge of their narrative, and the larger education conversation, by consciously crafting what they say, how they engage with others, and the story they choose to share" (Quaglia & Hamilton, 2015). The story of education is already being told—in part by frequent coverage in the news. However, the human tendency to gravitate toward the negative also applies to the press! The stories picked up highlight the challenges in schools more often than the successes. Teachers can use their voice to balance this story out, by also sharing about the amazing things happening in schools!

Teachers need to consider how they want to be perceived and start telling *their* stories. As Quaglia and Hamilton go on to say, it is important to note that "a teacher brand is not about having a cool logo or selling a product—it is a sincere representation of who you are as an educator." Developing a brand as a teacher is an opportunity to put a stake in the ground and declare it to anyone that will listen. Teachers should articulate the reason why they chose this profession and what energizes them about teaching. They should share their hopes and dreams for themselves as professionals, the students they teach, their school, and their community. Others will listen and can learn from teachers' stories. When teachers lead in this manner, they will bring balance to the current story of education often found in the press.

In addition to establishing a brand, teachers will make an impact with the digital footprint they create as they engage in the virtual world. Conversations around digital citizenship for students are increasing, but guidelines for teachers also need to be considered. Everything that is "said" in a digital space has a life expectancy of forever. The ease with which voice can be entered into the virtual world is not an indication that it should be taken lightly! On the contrary, the importance and tone of a message should be greatly considered given the lasting impact of the words.

To help with this, there are sites designed for the purpose of guiding students, teachers, and parents in issues related to digital safety and responsibility. One example is Commonsensemedia.org, which has an education section that includes videos, professional development with archived webinars, and educator blogs where you can ask questions and join the conversation about digital footprints in education.

Many districts and schools are creating system-level policies around the use of technology and social media. Steven Anderson (2016) is a former classroom teacher who now dedicates his professional efforts to supporting the infusion of technology in teaching and social medial in learning. The following are some of the guidelines and best practices he helped Kimmel Farm Elementary School develop for safely using social media in an educational setting.

- Don't tell secrets.
- Protect your own privacy.
- Be honest.
- Respect copyright laws.
- Be the first to respond to your own mistakes.
- Think about consequences.
- Utilize disclaimers.
- Do not forget your day job.
- Quality matters.

To learn more, check out the full policy, which is posted on Steven's Connected Classroom blog, along with additional resources related to technology and the concept of a connected classroom at http://blog.web20classroom.org/

Teachers should be mindful of the digital footprint that remains, but they should not let fear be a roadblock to the benefits of engaging their voice in virtual spaces. As always, teachers should consider their audience and be respectful—of others, themselves, and differing viewpoints. Share in a way that you can be proud of forever, because that is how long the footprint lasts!

CONVERSE, CREATE, AND CONTRIBUTE

Leveraging technology may start with conversations that amplify teacher voice, but it should naturally parlay into creating resources that reflect teachers' best practices and contributing those resources and associated insights to be used and learned from by others. The impact of teacher-generated ideas, resources, and strategies can, in ever-increasing ways, extend beyond the confines of individual classrooms to a global audience.

Listening to and learning from the myriad of conversations available via the Internet and social media can be of great personal and professional benefit. Teachers need to jump in and join the conversation! Every teacher has valuable ideas to share, and they should take the time to listen to and learn from each other. Joining existing conversations is valuable, but it is also beneficial to step up and lead a conversation. Teachers can lead a Twitter chat, start a dialogue through the communication channels in their school, conduct a webcast, or write a blog. Regardless of the channel of communication, this will help amplify their voice.

Our friend and colleague Peter DeWitt, a former teacher and principal, leads conversations with over 85,000 readers each week through his Education Week Blog *Finding Common Ground*. Dewitt is a consistent advocate for valuing the voices of educators and engages a wide variety of perspectives in the conversations sparked by his weekly blogs which can be found at http://blogs.edweek.org/edweek/finding_common_ground/.

Another example is found in the voice of Vicki Davis. She is a full time teacher who writes a blog called Cool Cat Teacher, which can be found at http://www.coolcatteacher.com/. As stated on her website, Davis is passionate about helping all teachers reach every student. She writes about teaching, staying motivated, connecting with other teachers, using technology effectively, and staying up to date on current news and trends in education.

We are also joining and leading virtual conversations in our own practice at the Quaglia Institute for School Voice and Aspirations. We offer a monthly webinar that is open to anyone interested in joining the conversation about School Voice. There is no official presentation, and no PowerPoint slides are unveiled. Teachers, administrators, and other stakeholders from around the world simply come together once a month to share their best practices and challenges. Utilizing a platform called Shindig, participants are able to converse in small groups, share resources, and take the "stage" as the presenter. We facilitate the conversation, but it is the voices of educators in the field that drive this collaboration. Educators from Dubai to California to England to South Carolina are able to meaningfully connect on a common topic of interest and passion: amplifying School Voice! Join the conversation at http://quagliainstitute.org.

TEACHER VOICE

Teacher voice can be powerful when combined with technology. Using Twitter for book studies and professional development allows teachers to listen to and talk with one another on various topics. I recently approached my principal about the possibility of having monthly Twitter Chats on topics that *teachers want* (we have a survey for teachers on possible topics). Giving teachers the choice on the hot topics to discuss will help them be more willing to connect on Twitter with other teachers. The chats will be teacher led and moderated; administrators can join in too . . . but as an equal voice.

Kelly Jones
3rd Grade Teacher
East Side Elementary School
Cobb County
Georgia

Building on their conversations, teachers can utilize technology to create classroom resources. The best teachers we know are continually creating new activities and learning tools for their students. Sometimes the creation is a completely novel idea, and sometimes it stems from an idea learned from a colleague. Other times the idea is wholeheartedly borrowed and implemented; yet that very idea can unfold differently in each classroom, and that may lead to a new insight that could help others. No teacher should keep these treasures hidden!

A wide variety of platforms exist to help teachers share resources and contribute to the education community, both within the walls of their building and beyond. Many school districts utilize GoogleDocs to foster the collaborative sharing of teacher resources, and Pinterest has become a go-to for many. Teachers Pay Teachers has also gained significant traction in attracting teachers seeking to locate or share classroom resources. Any teacher can post a resource they have created and can determine if they want to make it available for free or for a price determined by the individual teacher. Teachers themselves monitor the quality of resources as they utilize, review, and rate the content. EdShelf is another platform that facilitates the sharing of teacher-generated resources. Refined search options that allow teachers to find a lesson, activity, or resource directly matching what they are seeking are of great value.

Teachers should let their voices be heard and use technology to tell the story of who they are as educators! It may start locally, with teachers sharing their educational genius with fellow practitioners, but teachers conversing, creating, and contributing can amplify voice to create a more global impact. It is time for all teachers to listen, learn, and LEAD!

TEACHER VOICE

I had joined a Yahoo group for support and ideas on a reading program. It was wonderful sharing ideas across the country. I realized that I could start something similar. I began an e-mail collaboration group specific to my grade. Every time I attended a workshop or meeting, I asked other teachers at the same grade level for their e-mail addresses. Word spread. Teachers shared ideas and files. I asked for a district collaboration site to share our files. Today, we are three hundred strong and are working smarter, not harder. We now have planning sessions to address concerns and problem solve to address needs. E-mails fly fast and furious with materials to share. Our district has taken notice and encourages other grade levels to follow our lead. We now have a shared voice and a means to address our concerns in a proactive manner. As teachers, we are no longer isolated; we are strong.

Dana Jacobsen
First Grade Teacher
Spruce Creek Elementary
Volusia County Schools
Florida

AMPLIFYING TEACHER VOICE THROUGH TECHNOLOGY

Listen	• Develop a Professional Learning Network.
	• Listen to a webcast.
	• Follow a blog.
Learn	• Engage in a Twitter chat.
	• Filter and personalize online searches for information.
	• Reach out to experts and become one.
Lead	• Start a virtual conversation.
	• Establish a brand as a teacher.
	• Create and share resources in virtual spaces.

TEACHER VOICE: MAKE IT ROAR!

Teachers have a voice with or without technology. But that voice can grow from a whisper to a roar by leveraging technology. The distance your voice can travel and the range of influence can expand exponentially when teachers engage in the digital world. New avenues are opened up, locally and around the world.

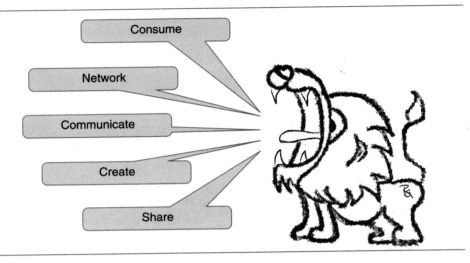

Teachers should remember to exercise moderation as they venture into virtual spaces. It is still critically important that teacher voice is expressed and valued in local contexts and that face-to-face collaborations are also maintained. It is important to avoid the potential pitfall of overdependency on technology! Engagement in community conversations, phone calls to parents, and meeting over coffee with colleagues are just a few examples of significant ways for teachers to utilize their voice outside of technology. Moderation!

TEACHER VOICE

When I communicate with parents, I use both e-mail and text. I think it is important to not focus only on negatives with parents, so I routinely send "good news" e-mails about A's on tests and positive behavior in class. I also use the Remind app to send reminders to students and parents. This helps my students stay on track, but also helps their parents, too, as high school is typically when students launch their independence. I also encourage conferences with parents and their children as it is important for parents to feel like their voices are heard, too.

Hillary Johnson
High School Biology Teacher
Lassiter High School
Cobb County School District
Marietta, Georgia

There are undoubtedly trends in education that come and go, but rest assured, technology is here to stay. It is not a fad or a gadget. Technology is now an integral part of daily life, and it serves teachers well to embrace it. The choice around technology should not be *if* you are going to use it, but *how well*.

There are endless books on how to use technology in the classroom to make learning more engaging. There is technology designed to make work in the area of assessment and evaluation allegedly easier. There is technology available that will provide information more quickly than it takes to ask for it. That is all fine and dandy, but this chapter is about how *teachers* can use technology in a way that will enhance their voice and give them the volume they need to be heard by and collaborate with others.

It is imperative that teachers learn to use technology to amplify their voice, celebrating their success, collaboratively determine solutions for their challenges, and help others understand what is important when it comes to school improvement efforts.

In short, and in technology terms, it is time for teacher voice to go viral! (In fishing terms, it's time to cast a wider net.)

Action Steps to Amplify Teacher Voice via Technology

- **Develop new Professional Learning Networks (PLNs).** PLNs are a fantastic way to amplify teacher voice. Twitter is an easy place to start. (And keep in mind that the younger generations are a great resource for assistance with technology!) Follow us at @DrRussQ and @Lisa_Lande, and join the conversation about teacher voice at @TVMatters.

- **Expand existing PLNs.** Adding new people and resources to existing PLNs serves to enhance professional growth and increases the influence of teacher voice. It is important to include varying viewpoints and perspective from other fields of expertise.

- **Reach out to experts.** Identify experts in areas related to your professional context. Visit their websites, follow them on social media, and do not be afraid to contact an expert directly. Whether or not a personal response is received (and it does happen!), the dialogue and learning with others who are interested in this expert's work can be beneficial.

- **Listen with intent to genuinely learn.** When listening to others, really focus on practicing effective listening skills. Do not think about responses while the other person is still talking! Really focus on what is being said and what can be learned from it.

- **Try something new.** No matter an educator's level of expertise, there is always more that can be learned. Seek out new resources and implement new strategies. TeachersPayTeachers.com is a great starting point.

- **Do not just consume, contribute.** Develop your ability to lead by using your voice in virtual spaces. Do more than read the comments in a Twitter chat; tweet your own thoughts. Start a blog and invite colleagues to read and comment. Post a resource you have created on Pinterest, TeachersPayTeachers.com, EdShelf, or another resource sharing site. Get involved with the EdCamp movement. Dream up an idea far beyond the possibilities currently imagined.

- **Thank someone and help someone.** We all have our go-to people that help us with technology issues. Thank someone who frequently helps you, and then seek out opportunities to help others strengthen their ability to use technology as a vehicle for amplifying their voice. Invite a colleague to join you for an #edchat conversation.

- **Establish a teacher brand.** Teachers need to articulate what they are passionate about and what makes them exceptional as educators. Teachers should share their hopes and dreams to tell their story!

- **Maintain moderation.** As fabulous as it is, remember that technology is not the be-all and end-all. Continue to listen, learn, and lead outside of virtual spaces. Human interaction is important. There is something about live conversations that builds relationships in a way that technology cannot replicate. Be sure to build relationships in the school and community.

Teacher Reflections

1. What types of perspectives do you listen to in your professional learning network? Are they diverse enough? How are these voices positively contributing to you achieving your aspirations?

2. Do you listen with a true intent to learn? How can you improve your listening skills?

3. What is your teacher brand? Do others know *who* you are and what makes you special as an educator?

4. What actions can you take to amplify your voice by leveraging technology?

CHAPTER 7

It Is Time for *Your* Voice to Be Heard

The sweetest of all sounds is when you use your voice to make a difference.

Our goal for this book is to provide teachers with the knowledge and skills they need to utilize their voice in meaningful ways within their school and community. It is a starting point for you, the teachers, based on research, years of experience, firsthand observations, and discussions with some of the best and brightest educators. Consider this your launching pad, the first step in your teacher voice journey. (Dare we say, the favorite spot from which you shall cast?) Each of your journey's will be different, but with a common goal—making meaningful improvement in education.

We have described the conditions that need to be in place for your voice to be heard. Within an atmosphere of trust, respect, and shared responsibility, teacher voice will thrive. Organizations have the responsibility to be ready and willing to hear the voices of teachers, and you must be ready and willing to express your voice. Permeating all these efforts must be a commitment from everyone to collaboratively foster teacher voice, incorporate it in meaningful decision making, and bring about positive change.

We presented data from thousands of teachers and shared insights from teachers who have learned and flourished through their experience of sharing their voice.

And we have asked you to reflect on who you are as a teacher, a leader, and an influencer within and beyond your school. You are a role model. That fact is not a choice; it is inherent in your position as a teacher. The choice you do have is determining what kind of role model you want to be—ultimately, how influential you will be as a leader. It is up to you to decide *how* and *how effectively* you will use your voice.

TEACHER VOICE

My priority is creating and maintaining individual relationships with my students. The key to their academic success is knowing that I see them individually rather than collectively . . . or worse, not at all. My voice is the quintessential component in successfully completing this task. My kids readily identify a difference in my voice—something they have not experienced frequently, if at all, in the past when interacting with teachers. Specifically, I talk *with* them rather than *at* them. What my students say, think, and feel matters to me; my voice genuinely communicates this, merging their worlds with mine through meaningful sharing and fostering a mutual respect.

Brent Jons
5th Grade Teacher
3 Years Teaching Experience
Pioneer Elementary
West Ada School District
Meridian, Idaho

Regardless of what is written in this book, simply reading it is not enough. It is up to *you* to take the next step—to exercise your voice in a way that will allow you to reach your fullest potential. Your voice is a catalyst for inspiration to students, colleagues, leadership, parents, and your community. You have the ability to raise the aspirations of your students by using your voice in a way that will motivate and encourage them to dream bigger and take the steps necessary to achieve those dreams.

We are advocating for a balanced expression of teacher voice that leads to engagement and action. This manifestation of voice is thoughtful, honest, and considerate of others. It is a confident voice, but one that can exercise self-restraint, frequently inviting the voices of others to join the conversation. Teachers with a balanced, engaged, and action-oriented voice are highly skilled in the art of communication and just as effective at listening as they are at speaking. Most importantly, the ideal voice is always focused on saying and doing what is best for the entire learning environment.

When teachers practice a balanced expression of voice, *all* voices are engaged, self-worth continually grows, and collective purpose is developed—all leading to meaningful action.

When Janet speaks, people listen. She is a highly skilled teacher and a gifted communicator. She manages to simultaneously exude confidence and humility. She is wise beyond her years but never comes across as a know-it-all. Janet is brutally honest at times, yet always kind and respectful. Her motive is clear: to create the most incredible learning experience possible for students. Janet never complains about challenges but continually seeks solutions to problems. Her voice is one of reason and value, always expressed with the good of the school community in mind. ■

AMPLIFYING SUCCESS

We can outline strategies for fostering teacher voice, provide common language for discussion, and encourage reflection to help determine effectiveness. But what matters most is that *every* individual in a school system works toward creating a school culture that honors and incorporates *every* teacher voice, in all forms of expression. All voices in a school community are worthy of being heard, both when they are at their best and when they are struggling.

In Chapter 4, we shared: "Student voice is the instrument of change. We are at a point when we and our students must stand up and be heard or the educational policy mongers will continue to strip us of the basic purpose of education, which is to allow our students to dream, reach, and succeed" (Quaglia & Corso, 2014, p. 174).

And we also shared a dream: *We dream of schools in which students and teachers both have voice; where they are not afraid to share their honest opinions and concerns, ask questions, and try new things; where they are learners, instructors, and advocates alongside one another and collaborating with one another; where they are afforded regular opportunities to listen, learn, and lead.*

This dream is possible, with student voice as the instrument of change and teacher voice as the tool to amplify success.

It is crucial for the individual voices of teachers to be heard in harmony—not in the sense that all ideas are the same and or even in sync but that the collaborative efforts honor discord and develop solutions that are beneficial to all. The shared goal is a learning environment that enriches the self-worth, engagement, and purpose of every stakeholder. It is unrealistic (and even unproductive) for everyone to be in perfect agreement. However, the harmony of their goals, and the mutual respect for their shared purpose, should create a perfect opportunity to amplify the success of the entire educational community.

TEACHER VOICE

Don't ask someone to do something if you are not willing to do it yourself. This year I decided to put those words into action. At the beginning of the year, I gave my students a survey, asking them to write down their reading goals and decide if they were willing to work toward their goals. I also set a goal for myself, and that was to run another marathon. I paralleled my running experience with their reading curriculum: how to set realistic goals, break down goals into manageable parts, and the importance of working toward that goal. One day a week, I will take my small group out to run for 40 minutes. While we are running, I will ask them text-dependent questions from the weekly story. I am hoping my voice will make a difference in their lives, showing my students that together, we can accomplish goals.

Debora Tarmann
ESE Teacher
Spruce Creek Elementary
Volusia County School District
Port Orange, Florida

If teachers are to strengthen their sense of purpose, they must *truly* lead in every aspect of school, from rethinking the effective use of time and schedules to teaching assignments to discipline procedures and school climate. Genuine leadership roles allow teachers to do more than provide token input. They allow teachers to take action and to assume responsibility for results. This kind of collaborative leadership is the key to teacher, student, and school success.

Teachers will always have a voice, but the scope of influence of that voice will be determined by teachers' resolve to share their voice and leadership's willingness to listen. When teacher voice is valued and acted upon, positive teacher voice will be heard by parents in the grocery stores and malls, innovative teacher voice will be heard by students in classrooms, insightful teacher voices will be posted on social media, and spirited teacher voice will be echoed and celebrated among the staff. When teachers' voices work in unison, great progress can happen.

To transform our schools, honoring and responding to teacher voice must become a natural way of being in schools; incorporating teacher voice must be an ongoing, sustained effort. This requires teachers to be vulnerable and thoughtful as ideas are challenged, and it demands that teachers and leadership alike accept diverse and radically different ideas without prejudging. After all, innovation always starts with something different!

We have said for years that students are not the problem; they are the potential. And so it is the case with teachers. Teachers have the responsibility to share their ideas in constructive ways, and schools have the responsibility to involve teacher voice. Making teacher voice part of the fabric of school culture has the potential to create meaningful and lasting improvements in the teaching and learning environment. When teacher voice is the norm, collaborative leadership efforts can move mountains!

It all boils down to three words (and the order matters): *Listen, learn,* and *lead.* Teachers must listen with the intent to understand, learn with the intent to grow, and lead with the intent to make a difference.

FOSTERING YOUR VOICE

Listen	• Seek out new ideas! Make an effort to listen to people you do not typically associate with on a regular basis.
	• Stay current on education issues in *and* outside your school community.
	• Be mindful of opportunities to collaborate; resist confrontation.
	• Be open to learning and understanding
Learn	• Be respectful of new and differing ideas.
	• Develop online professional relationships.
	• Believe that other people have something to teach you.
	• Ask questions for clarity.
Lead	• Understand who you are sharing your voice with and why.
	• Share your thoughts in a variety of forums, including every technological tool available.
	• Celebrate who you are and what you stand for as a professional. Be proud to be a teacher!
	• Work collaboratively with students, colleagues, leadership, parents, and the community to improve education for all.

The lessons learned from this book are meaningless if they lay dormant, and so we challenge you to get started:

- Believe in yourself; your ideas and opinions are important and deserve to be heard.

- Devote the patience and time necessary to genuinely listen to others.

- Seek out varying opinions to maximize learning.

- Be willing and brave enough to share your voice.

- Be proud and celebrate who you are as a professional and what you believe is best for students.

- Support the voices of students, colleagues, leaders, parents, and the community; each has something to teach you, and every collaborative effort presents an opportunity to lead together.

- Always remember that wonderful surprises are just waiting to happen. *YOUR* voice can be the agent of change!

As the final "t" is crossed and the last "i" dotted in this book, the chill is back in the air, the leaves have fallen off the trees, and the bite is off. Along with this book, the fishing season has come to a close. Gear is away, and it is time for reflection—celebrating triumphs and learning from the ones that got away.

Teachers, too, need to reflect, celebrate successes, and learn from mistakes. But the great thing is, you do not need to wait for a new season. Your voice is ready; start sharing, collaborating, and amplifying your successes *now!* Sometimes the first cast is the most difficult, but it always improves with practice . . . and perhaps a little patience and determination.

References

Alliance for Excellent Education. (2014, July). *On the path to equity: Improving the effectiveness of beginning teachers.* Retrieved from http://all4ed.org/wp-content/uploads/2014/07/PathToEquity.pdf

Anderson, S. (2016). Kimmel Farm social media guidelines and best practices [Web log]. Retrieved from http://blog.web20classroom.org/p/sample-social-media-guidelines.html

Bangs, J., & Frost, D. (2012). *Teacher self-efficacy, voice and leadership: Towards a policy framework for education international.* Brussels, Belgium: Education International Research Institute.

Berry, B., Byrd, A., & Wieder, A. (2013). *Teacherpreneurs: Innovative teachers who lead but don't leave.* San Francisco, CA: Jossey-Bass.

Collier, L. (2011). The need for teacher communities: An interview with Linda-Darling-Hammond. *The Council Chronicle, 14.*

Csikszentmihalyi, M. (1990). *Flow.* New York: Harper Perennial.

DeWitt, P. (in press). *Collaborative leadership: 6 influences that matter most.* Thousand Oaks, CA: Corwin.

Dolton, P., & Marcenaro-Gutierrez, O. (2013). *2013 Global Teacher Status Index.* Varkey GEMS Foundation. Retrieved from https://www.varkeyfoundation.org/sites/default/files/documents/2013GlobalTeacherStatusIndex.pdf

Damon, W. (2008). *The pathway to purpose: Helping our children find their calling in life.* New York: Harper & Row.

Danielson, C. (2007). The many faces of leadership. *Educational Leadership, 65*(1), 14–19.

Dweck, C. (2006). *Mindset: The new psychology of success.* New York: Random House.

Dweck, C., Walton, G., & Cohen, G. (2014). *Academic tenacity: Mindsets and skills that promote long-term learning.* Bill and Melinda Gates Foundation.

Every Student Succeeds Act. (2015, December). Retrieved from https://www.gpo.gov/fdsys/pkg/BILLS-114s1177enr/pdf/BILLS-114s1177enr.pdf

Fennell, M. (2016, January 7). Will ESSA offer new opportunities for educators? [Web blog]. Retrieved from http://blogs.edweek.org/teachers/teacher_leader_voices/2016/01/will_ essa_offer_new_leadership.html

Fox, K. (2015, April 17). Please . . . No more professional development! [Web blog]. Retrieved from http://blogs.edweek.org/edweek/finding_common_ground/2015/04/please_please_pleaseno_more_professional_development.html

Fullan, M., & Quinn, J. (2016). *Coherence: The right drivers in action for schools, districts, and systems.* Thousand Oaks, CA: Corwin.

Fullan, M., & Langworthy, M. (2014, January). *A rich seam: How pedagogies find deep learning*. London, England: Pearson. Retrieved from http://www.michaelfullan.ca/wp-content/uploads/2014/01/3897.Rich_Seam_web.pdf

Goulston, M. (2010). *Just listen: Discover the secret to getting through to absolutely anyone*. New York: Amacom.

Hargreaves, A. (1994). *Changing teachers, changing times: Teachers' work and culture in the postmodern age*. New York: Teachers College Press.

Hargreaves A., & Ainscow, M. (2015, November). The top and bottom of leadership change. *Phi Delta Kappan, 97*(3), 42–48.

Hargreaves, A., & Fullan, M. (2012). *Professional capital: Transforming teaching in every school*. New York, NY: Teachers College Press.

Hargreaves, A., & Fullan M. (2013). The power of professional capital. *JSD 34*(3), 36–39.

Hattie, J. (2003, October). *Teachers make a difference: What is the research evidence?* Paper presented at the Australian Council for Educational Research Annual Conference on Building Teacher Quality, Melbourne.

Hattie, J. (2009). *Visible learning: A synthesis of over 800 meta-analyses relating to achievement*. London: Routledge.

Hattie, J. (2012). *Visible learning for teachers: Maximizing impact on learning*. London: Routledge.

Hattie, J. (2015). *The power of collaborative expertise*. London: Pearson.

Heath, C., & Heath, D. (2010). *Switch: How to change things when change is hard*. New York: Broadway Books.

Kahn, G. (2014, January 2). The Amazon of higher education: How tiny, struggling New Hampshire University became a behemoth [Web log]. Retrieved from http://www.slate.com/articles/life/education/2014/01/southern_new_hampshire_university_how_paul_leblanc_s_tiny_school_has_become.html

Knight, J. (2011). *Unmistakable impact: A partnership approach for dramatically improving instruction*. Thousand Oaks, CA: Corwin.

Knight, J. (2016). *Better conversations: Coaching ourselves and each other to be more credible, caring, and connected*. Thousand Oaks, CA: Corwin.

MetLife. (2013). *The MetLife survey of the American teacher: Challenges for school leadership*. New York: Author.

Muhammad, A. (2009). *Transforming school culture: How to overcome staff division*. Bloomington, IN: Solution Tree Press.

OECD. (2013a). *TALIS 2013 results: An international perspective on teaching and learning*. Paris: OECD Publishing.

OECD. (2013b). *A teachers' guide to TALIS 2013*. Paris: OECD Publishing.

OECD. (2014, September). *Teaching in focus 5: What helps teachers feel valued and satisfied with their jobs*. Retrieved from http://www.oecd.org/edu/school/TIF5.pdf

Phillips, O. (2015, March 30). *Revolving door of teachers costs schools billions every year*. nprEd. Retrieved from http://www.npr.org/sections/ed/2015/03/30/395322012/the-hidden-costs-of-teacher-turnover

Quaglia, R. J. (2017). *Principal voice: Listen, learn, lead*. Thousand Oaks, CA: Corwin.

Quaglia, R. J., & Corso, M. J. (2014). *Student voice: The instrument of change*. Thousand Oaks, CA: Corwin.

Quaglia, R. J., & Hamilton, A. (2015, March 17). Making your voice heard: The power of the teacher brand [Web log]. Retrieved from http://blogs.edweek.org/edweek/finding_common_ground/2015/03/making_your_voice_heard_the_power_of_the_teacher_brand.html

Quaglia, R. J., & Lande, L. L. (2016). *Teacher voice: Understanding the dynamics of change.* Thousand Oaks, CA: Corwin Press.

Quaglia Institute for Student Aspirations. (2014). *My voice national student voice report (Grades 6–12).* Retrieved from http://www.qisa.org/dmsView/My_Voice_2013-2014_National_Report_8_25

Quaglia Institute for Student Aspirations, & Teacher Voice and Aspirations International Center. (2015). *Teacher Voice report 2010–2014.* Retrieved from http://www.qisa.org/dmsView/TeacherVoiceReport

Richardson, W., & Mancabelli, R. (2011). *Personal learning networks: Using the power of connections to transform education.* Bloomington, IN: Solution Tree.

Schmidt, E., & Cohen, J. (2013). *The new digital age: Reshaping the future of people nations and business.* New York: Knopf.

Sheninger, E. (2014). *Digital leadership: Changing paradigms for changing times.* Thousand Oaks, CA: Corwin.

Weinberger, D. (2011). *Too big to know: Rethinking knowledge now that the facts aren't the facts, experts are everywhere, and the smartest person in the room is the room.* New York: Basic Books.

Index

A SAGE Publishing Company

CORWIN HAS ONE MISSION: to enhance education through intentional professional learning.

We build long-term relationships with our authors, educators, clients, and associations who partner with us to develop and continuously improve the best evidence-based practices that establish and support lifelong learning.

Solutions you want. Experts you trust.
Results you need.

 **AUTHOR CONSULTING**

Author Consulting

On-site professional learning with sustainable results! Let us help you design a professional learning plan to meet the unique needs of your school or district. www.corwin.com/pd

 **INSTITUTES**

Institutes

Corwin Institutes provide collaborative learning experiences that equip your team with tools and action plans ready for immediate implementation. www.corwin.com/institutes

eCOURSES

eCourses

Practical, flexible online professional learning designed to let you go at your own pace. www.corwin.com/ecourses

READ2EARN

Read2Earn

Did you know you can earn graduate credit for reading this book? Find out how: www.corwin.com/read2earn

Contact an account manager at (800) 831-6640 or visit
www.corwin.com for more information.

 CORWIN